ISBN 0-8373-2774-1

C-2774   **CAREER EXAMINATION SERIES**

This is your PASSBOOK® for...

Golf Course Supervisor

Test Preparation Study Guide

Questions & Answers

NLC

NATIONAL LEARNING CORPORATION

Copyright © 2009 by

National Learning Corporation

212 Michael Drive, Syosset, New York 11791

All rights reserved, including the right of reproduction in whole or in part, in any form or by any means, electronic or mechanical, including photocopying, recording, or by any information storage and retrieval system, without permission in writing from the Publisher.

(516) 921-8888
(800) 645-6337
FAX: (516) 921-8743
www.passbooks.com
sales @ passbooks.com
info @ passbooks.com

PRINTED IN THE UNITED STATES OF AMERICA

PASSBOOK®
NOTICE

This book is *SOLELY* intended for, is sold *ONLY* to, and its use is *RESTRICTED* to *individual*, bona fide applicants or candidates who qualify by virtue of having seriously filed applications for appropriate license, certificate, professional and/or promotional advancement, higher school matriculation, scholarship, or other legitimate requirements of educational and/or governmental authorities.

This book is *NOT* intended for use, class instruction, tutoring, training, duplication, copying, reprinting, excerption, or adaptation, etc., by:

(1) Other publishers

(2) Proprietors and/or Instructors of "Coaching" and/or Preparatory Courses

(3) Personnel and/or Training Divisions of commercial, industrial, and governmental organizations

(4) Schools, colleges, or universities and/or their departments and staffs, including teachers and other personnel

(5) Testing Agencies or Bureaus

(6) Study groups which seek by the purchase of a single volume to copy and/or duplicate and/or adapt this material for use by the group as a whole without having purchased individual volumes for each of the members of the group

(7) Et al.

Such persons would be in violation of appropriate Federal and State statutes.

PROVISION OF LICENSING AGREEMENTS. — Recognized educational commercial, industrial, and governmental institutions and organizations, and others legitimately engaged in educational pursuits, including training, testing, and measurement activities, may address a request for a licensing agreement to the copyright owners, who will determine whether, and under what conditions, including fees and charges, the materials in this book may be used by them. In other words, a licensing facility exists for the legitimate use of the material in this book on other than an individual basis. However, it is asseverated and affirmed here that the material in this book *CANNOT* be used without the receipt of the express permission of such a licensing agreement from the Publishers.

NATIONAL LEARNING CORPORATION
212 Michael Drive
Syosset, New York 11791

Inquiries re licensing agreements should be addressed to:
The President
National Learning Corporation
212 Michael Drive
Syosset, New York 11791

PASSBOOK SERIES®

THE *PASSBOOK SERIES*® has been created to prepare applicants and candidates for the ultimate academic battlefield—the examination room.

At some time in our lives, each and every one of us may be required to take an examination—for validation, matriculation, admission, qualification, registration, certification, or licensure.

Based on the assumption that every applicant or candidate has met the basic formal educational standards, has taken the required number of courses, and read the necessary texts, the *PASSBOOK SERIES*® furnishes the one special preparation which may assure passing with confidence, instead of failing with insecurity. Examination questions—together with answers—are furnished as the basic vehicle for study so that the mysteries of the examination and its compounding difficulties may be eliminated or diminished by a sure method.

This book is meant to help you pass your examination provided that you qualify and are serious in your objective.

The entire field is reviewed through the huge store of content information which is succinctly presented through a provocative and challenging approach—the question-and-answer method.

A climate of success is established by furnishing the correct answers at the end of each test.

You soon learn to recognize types of questions, forms of questions, and patterns of questioning. You may even begin to anticipate expected outcomes.

You perceive that many questions are repeated or adapted so that you gain acute insights, which may enable you to score many sure points.

You learn how to confront new questions, or types of questions, and to attack them confidently and work out the correct answers.

You note objectives and emphases, and recognize pitfalls and dangers, so that you may make positive educational adjustments.

Moreover, you are kept fully informed in relation to new concepts, methods, practices, and directions in the field.

You discover that you are actually taking the examination all the time: you are preparing for the examination by "taking" an examination, not by reading extraneous and/or supererogatory textbooks.

In short, this PASSBOOK®, used directedly, should be an important factor in helping you to pass your test.

GOLF COURSE SUPERVISOR

DUTIES

Supervises and schedules the work of clerical, custodial, and maintenance personnel at a golf course. Supervises the collection of golf course fees and maintenance of necessary accounting records. Enforces golf course rules and regulations personally and through subordinate staff. Makes regular inspections to ensure the maintenance of golf course and park facilities in a clean and sanitary condition. Participates in and supervises a variety of maintenance and repair activities involving the golf course and general park facilities including buildings and grounds.

SCOPE OF THE WRITTEN TEST

The written test will be designed to test knowledge, skills, and/or abilities in such areas as:
1. Record keeping;
2. Building cleaning, operation, and maintenance; and
3. Supervision.

HOW TO TAKE A TEST

I. YOU MUST PASS AN EXAMINATION

   A. WHAT EVERY CANDIDATE SHOULD KNOW

   Examination applicants often ask us for help in preparing for the written test. What can I study in advance? What kinds of questions will be asked? How will the test be given? How will the papers be graded?

   As an applicant for a civil service examination, you may be wondering about some of these things. Our purpose here is to suggest effective methods of advance study and to describe civil service examinations.

   Your chances for success on this examination can be increased if you know how to prepare. Those "pre-examination jitters" can be reduced if you know what to expect. You can even experience an adventure in good citizenship if you know why civil service examinations are given.

   B. WHY ARE CIVIL SERVICE EXAMINATIONS GIVEN?

   Civil service examinations are important to you in two ways. As a citizen, you want public jobs filled by employees who know how to do their work. As a job-seeker, you want a fair chance to compete for that job on an equal footing with other candidates. The best known means of accomplishing this two-fold goal is the competitive examination.

   Examinations are widely publicized throughout the nation. They may be administered for jobs in federal, state, city, municipal, town, or village governments or agencies.

   Any citizen may apply, with some limitations, such as the age or residence of applicants. Your experience and education may be reviewed to see whether you meet the requirements for the particular examination. When these requirements exist, they are reasonable and are applied consistently to all applicants. Thus, a competitive examination may cause you some uneasiness now, but it is your privilege and safeguard.

   C. HOW ARE CIVIL SERVICE EXAMINATIONS DEVELOPED?

   Examinations are carefully written by trained technicians who are specialists in the field known as "psychological measurement," in consultation with recognized authorities in the field of work that the test will cover. These experts recommend the subject matter areas or skills to be tested; only those knowledges or skills important to your success on the job are included. The most reliable books and source materials available are used as references. Together, the experts and technicians judge the difficulty level of the questions.

   Test technicians know how to phrase questions so that the problem is clearly stated. Their ethics do not permit "trick" or "catch" questions. Questions may have been tried out on sample groups, or subjected to statistical analysis, to determine their usefulness.

   Written tests are often used in combination with performance tests, ratings of training and experience, and oral interviews. All of these measures combine to form the best known means of finding the right man for the right job.

II. HOW TO PASS THE WRITTEN TEST

A. *NATURE OF THE EXAMINATION*

To prepare intelligently for civil service examinations, you should know how they differ from school examinations you have taken. In school you were assigned certain definite pages to read or subjects to cover. The examination questions were quite detailed and usually emphasized memory. Civil service examinations, on the other hand, try to discover your present ability to perform the duties of a position, plus your potentiality to learn these duties. In other words, a civil service examination attempts to predict how successful you will be. Questions cover such a broad area that they cannot be as minute and detailed as school examination questions.

In the public service similar kinds of work, or positions, are grouped together in one "class." This process is known as "position-classification." All the positions in a class are paid according to the salary range for that class. One class title covers all these positions, and they are all tested by the same examination.

B. *FOUR BASIC STEPS*

1. Study the Announcement.--How, then, can you know what subjects to study? Our best answer is: "Learn as much as possible about the class of positions for which you have applied." The examination will test the knowledge, skills, and abilities needed to do the work.

Your most valuable source of information about the position you want is the official announcement of the examination. This announcement lists the training and experience qualifications. Check these standards and apply only if you come reasonably close to meeting them.

The brief description of the position in the examination announcement offers some clues to the subjects which will be tested. Think about the job itself. Review the duties in your mind. Can you perform them, or are there some in which you are rusty? Fill in the blank spots in your preparation.

Many jurisdictions preview the written test in the examination announcement by including a section called "Knowledge and Abilities Required," "Scope of Examination," or some similar heading. Here you will find out specifically what fields will be tested.

2. Review Your Own Background.-- Once you learn in general what the position is all about, and what you need to know to do the work, ask yourself which subjects you already know fairly well and which need improvement. You may wonder whether to concentrate on improving your strong areas or on building some background in your fields of weakness. When the announcement has specified "some knowledge" or "considerable knowledge," or has used adjectives such as "beginning principles of ...." or "advanced .....methods," you can get a clue as to the number and difficulty of questions to be asked in any given field. More questions, and hence broader coverage, would be included for those subjects which are more important in the work. Now weigh your strengths and weaknesses against the job requirements and prepare accordingly.

3. Determine the Level of the Position.-- Another way to tell how intensively you should prepare is to understand the level of the job for which you are applying. Is it the entering level? In other words, is this the position in which beginners in a field of work are hired? Or is it an intermediate or advanced level? Sometimes this is indicated by such words as "Junior" or "Senior" in the class title. Other jurisdictions use Roman numerals to designate the level: Clerk I,

Clerk II, for example. The word "Supervisor" sometimes appears in the title. If the level is not indicated by the title, check the description of duties. Will you be working under very close supervision, or will you have responsibility for independent decisions in this work?

    4. Choose Appropriate Study Materials.-- Now that you know the subjects to be examined and the relative amount of each subject to be covered, you can choose suitable study materials. For beginning level jobs, or even advanced ones, if you have a pronounced weakness in some aspect of your training, read a modern, standard textbook in that field. Be sure it is up-to-date and has general coverage. Such books are normally available at your library, and the librarian will be glad to help you locate one. For entry level positions, questions of appropriate difficulty are chosen -- neither highly advanced questions, nor those too simple. Such questions require careful thought but not advanced training.

    If the position for which you are applying is technical or advanced, you will read more advanced, specialized material. If you are already familiar with the basic principles of your field, elementary textbooks would waste your time. Concentrate on advanced textbooks and technical periodicals. Think through the concepts and review difficult problems in your field.

    These are all general sources. You can get more ideas on your own initiative, following these leads. For example, training manuals and publications of the government agency which employs workers in your field can be useful, particularly for technical and professional positions. A letter or visit to the government department involved may result in more specific study suggestions, and certainly will provide you with a more definite idea of the exact nature of the position you are seeking.

II. KINDS OF TESTS

Tests are used for purposes other than measuring knowledge and ability to perform specified duties. For some positions, it is equally important to test ability to make adjustments to new situations or to profit from training. In others, basic mental abilities not dependent upon information are essential. Questions which test these things may not appear as pertinent to the duties of the position as those which test for knowledge and information. Yet they are often highly important parts of a fair examination. For very general questions, it is almost impossible to help you direct your study efforts. What we can do is to point out some of the more common of these general abilities needed in public service positions and describe some typical questions.

  1. General Information

    Broad, general information has been found useful for predicting job success in some kinds of work. This is tested in a variety of ways, from vocabulary lists to questions about current events. Basic background in some field of work, such as sociology or economics, may be sampled in a group of questions. Often these are principles which have become familiar to most persons through "exposure" rather than through formal training. It is difficult to advise you how to study for these questions; being alert to the world around you is our best suggestion.

2. Verbal Ability

An example of an ability needed in many positions is verbal or language ability. Verbal ability is, in brief, the ability to use and understand words. Vocabulary and grammar tests are typical measures of this ability. "Reading comprehension" or "paragraph interpretation" questions are common in many kinds of civil service tests. You are given a paragraph of written material and asked to find its central meaning.

3. Numerical Ability

Number skills can be tested by the familiar arithmetic problem, by checking paired lists of numbers to see which are alike and which are different, or by interpreting charts and graphs. In the latter test, a graph may be printed in the test booklet which you are asked to use as the basis for answering questions.

4. Observation

A popular test for law-enforcement positions is the observation test. A picture is shown to you for several minutes, then taken away. Questions about the picture test your ability to observe both details and larger elements.

5. Following Directions

In many positions in the public service, the employee must be able to carry out written instructions dependably and accurately. You may be given a chart with several columns, each column listing a variety of information. The questions require you to carry out directions involving the information given in the chart.

6. Skills and Aptitudes

Performance tests effectively measure some manual skills and aptitudes. When the skill is one in which you are trained, such as typing or shorthand, you can practice. These tests are often very much like those given in business school or high school courses. For many of the other skills and aptitudes, however, no short-time preparation can be made. Skills and abilities natural to you or that you have developed throughout your lifetime are being tested.

Many of the general questions just described provide all the data needed to answer the questions and ask you to use your reasoning ability to find the answers. Your best preparation for these tests, as well as for tests of facts and ideas, is to be at your physical and mental best. You, no doubt, have your own methods of getting into an exam-taking mood and keeping "in shape." The next section lists some ideas on this subject.

IV. KINDS OF QUESTIONS

Only rarely is the "essay" question, which you answer in narrative form, used in civil service tests. Civil service tests are usually of the short-answer type. Full instructions for answering these questions will be given to you at the examination. But in case this is your first experience with short-answer questions and separate answer sheets, here is what you need to know.

1. Multiple-Choice Questions

Most popular of the short-answer questions is the "multiple-choice" or "best-answer" question. It can be used, for example, to test for factual knowledge, ability to solve problems, or judgment in meeting situations found at work.

A multiple-choice question is normally one of three types:

(1) It can begin with an incomplete statement followed by several possible endings. You are to find the one ending which *best* completes the statement, although some of the others may not be entirely wrong.

(2) It can also be a complete statement in the form of a question which is answered by choosing one of the statements listed.

(3) It can be in the form of a problem -- again you select the best answer.

Here is an example of a multiple-choice question with a discussion which should give you some clues as to the method for choosing the right answer.

SAMPLE QUESTION:

When an employee has a complaint about his assignment, the action which will *best* help him overcome his difficulty is

(A) to discuss his difficulty with his co-workers
(B) to take the problem to the head of the organization
(C) to take the problem to the person who gave him the assignment
(D) to say nothing to anyone about his complaint

In answering this question you should study each of the choices to find which is best. Consider choice (A). Certainly an employee may discuss his complaint with fellow employees, but no change or improvement can result, and the complaint remains unsolved. Choice (B) is a poor choice since the head of the organization probably does not know what assignment you have been given, and taking your problem to him is known as "going over the head" of the supervisor. The supervisor, or person who made the assignment, is the person who can clarify it or correct any injustice. Choice (C) is, therefore, correct. To say nothing, as in choice (D), is unwise. Supervisors have an interest in knowing the problems employees are facing, and the employee is seeking a solution to his problem.

2. True-False Questions

The "true-false" or "right-wrong" form of question is sometimes used. Here a complete statement is given. Your problem is to decide whether the statement is right or wrong.

SAMPLE QUESTION:

A person-to-person long distance telephone call costs less than a station-to-station call to the same city.

This question is wrong, or "false," since person-to-person calls are more expensive.

This is not a complete list of all possible question forms, although most of the others are variations of these common types. You will always get complete directions for answering questions. Be sure you understand *how* to mark your answers -- ask questions until you do.

V. RECORDING YOUR ANSWERS

For an examination with very few applicants, you may be told to record your answers in the test booklet itself. Separate answer sheets are much more common. If this separate answer sheet is to be scored by machine -- and this is often the case -- it is highly important that you mark your answers correctly in order to get credit.

An electric test-scoring machine is often used in civil service offices because of the speed with which papers can be scored. Machine-scored answer sheets must be marked with a special pencil, which will be given to you. This pencil has a high graphite content which responds to the electrical scoring machine. As a matter of fact, stray dots may register as answers, so do not let your pencil rest on the answer sheet while you are pondering the correct answer. Also, if your pencil lead breaks or is otherwise defective, ask for another.

Since the answer sheet will be dropped in a slot in the scoring machine, be careful not to bend the corners or get the paper crumpled.

The answer sheet normally has five vertical columns of numbers, with 30 numbers to a column. These numbers correspond to the question numbers in your test booklet. After each number, going across the page, are four or five pairs of dotted lines. These short dotted lines have small letters or numbers above them. The first two pairs may also have a "T" and "F" above the letters. This indicates that the first two pairs only are to be used if the questions are of the true-false type. If the questions are multiple-choice, disregard this "T" and "F" completely, and pay attention only to the small number or letters.

Answer your questions in the manner of the sample that follows. Proceed in the sequential steps outlined below.

Assume that you are answering question 32, which is:
   32. The largest city in the United States is:
      A. Washington, D.C.   B. New York City   C. Chicago
      D. Detroit   E. San Francisco

1. Choose the answer you think is best.
    New York City is the largest, so choice B is correct.
2. Find the row of dotted lines numbered the same as the question you are answering.
    This is question number 32, so find row number 32.
3. Find the pair of dotted lines corresponding to the answer you have chosen.
    You have chosen answer B, so find the pair of dotted lines marked "B".
4. Make a solid black mark between the dotted lines.
    Go up and down two or three times with your pencil so plenty of graphite rubs off, but do not let the mark get outside or above the dots.

VI. BEFORE THE TEST

Common sense will help you find procedures to follow to get ready for an examination. Too many of us, however, overlook these sensible measures. Indeed, nervousness and fatigue have been found to be the most serious reasons why applicants fail to do their best on civil service tests. Here is a list of reminders.

1. Begin Your Preparation Early
    Don't wait until the last minute to go scurrying around for books and materials or to find out what the position is all about.
2. Prepare Continuously
    An hour a night for a week is better than an all-night cram session. This has been definitely established. What is more, a night a week for a month will return better dividends than crowding your study into a shorter period of time.
3. Locate the Place of the Examination
    You have been sent a notice telling you when and where to report for the examination. If the location is in a different town or otherwise unfamiliar to you, it would be well to inquire the best route and learn something about the building.
4. Relax the Night Before the Test
    Allow your mind to rest. Do not study at all that night. Plan some mild recreation or diversion; then go to bed early and get a good night's sleep.
5. Get Up Early Enough to Make a Leisurely Trip to the Place for the Test
    Then unforeseen events, traffic snarls, unfamiliar buildings, will not upset you.
6. Dress Comfortably
    A written test is not a fashion show. You will be known by number and not by name, so wear something comfortable.
7. Leave Excess Paraphernalia at Home
    Shopping bags and odd bundles will get in your way. You need bring only the items mentioned in the official notice sent to you; usually everything you need is provided. Do not bring reference books to the examination. They will only confuse those last minutes and be taken away from you when in the test room.
8. Arrive Somewhat Ahead of Time
    If because of transportation schedules you must get there very early, bring a newspaper or magazine to take your mind off yourself while waiting.
9. Locate the Examination Room
    When you have found the proper room, you will be directed to the seat or part of the room where you will sit. Sometimes you are given a sheet of instructions to read while you are waiting. Do not fill out any forms until you are told to do so; just read them and be ready.
10. Relax and Prepare to Listen to the Instructions
11. If you have any physical problem that may keep you from doing your best, be sure to tell the test administrator. If you are sick, or in poor health, you really cannot do your best on the test. You can come back and take the test some other time.

II. AT THE TEST

The day of the test is here and you have the test booklet in your hand. The temptation to get going is very strong. Caution! There is more to success than knowing the right answers. You must know how to identify your papers and understand variations in the type of short-answer question used in this particular examination. Follow these suggestions for maximum results from your efforts:

1. Cooperate with the Monitor

The test administrator has a duty to create a situation in which you can be as much at ease as possible. He will give instructions, tell you when to begin, check to see that you are marking your answer sheet correctly. He is not there to guard you, although he will see that your competitors do not take unfair advantage. He wants to help you do your best.

2. Listen to All Instructions

Don't jump the gun! Wait until you understand all directions. In most civil service tests you get more time than you need to answer the questions. So don't get in a hurry. Read each word of instructions until you clearly understand the meaning. Study the examples. Listen to all announcements. Follow directions. Ask questions if you do not understand what to do.

3. Identify Your Papers

Civil service examinations are usually identified by number only. You will be assigned a number; you must not put your name on your test papers. Be sure to copy your number correctly. Since more than one examination may be given, copy your exact examination title.

4. Plan Your Time

Unless you are told that a test is a "speed" or "rate-of-work" test, speed itself is not usually important. Time enough to answer all the questions will be provided. But this does not mean that you have all day. An overall time limit has been set. Divide the total time (in minutes) by the number of questions to get the approximate time you have for each question.

5. Do Not Linger Over Difficult Questions

If you come across a difficult question, mark it with a paper clip (useful to have along) and come back to it when you have been through the booklet. One caution if you do this -- be sure to skip a number on your answer sheet too. Check often to be sure that you have not lost your place and that you are marking in the row numbered the same as the question you are answering.

6. Read the Questions

Be sure you know what the question asks! Many capable people are unsuccessful because they failed to *read* the questions correctly.

7. Answer All Questions

Unless you have been instructed that a penalty will be deducted for incorrect answers, it is better to guess than to omit a question.

8. Speed Tests

It is often better *not* to guess on speed tests. It has been found that on timed tests people are tempted to spend the last few seconds before time is called in marking answers at random -- without even reading them -- in the hope of picking up a few extra points. To discourage this practice, the instructions may warn you that your score will be "corrected" for guessing. That is, a penalty will be applied. The incorrect answers will be deducted from the correct ones, or some other penalty formula will be used.

9. Review Your Answers

If you finish before time is called, go back to the questions you guessed or omitted to give further thought to them. Review other answers if you have time.

10. Return Your Test Materials

If you are ready to leave before others have finished or time is called, take *all* your materials to the monitor and leave quietly. Never take any test material with you. The monitor can discover whose papers are not complete, and taking a test booklet may be grounds for disqualification.

III. EXAMINATION TECHNIQUES

1. Read the *general* instructions carefully. These are usually printed on the first page of the examination booklet. As a rule, these instructions refer to the timing of the examination; the fact that you should not start work until the signal and must stop work at a signal, etc. If there are any *special* instructions, such as a choice of questions to be answered, make sure that you note this instruction carefully.

2. When you are ready to start work on the examination, that is as soon as the signal has been given, read the instructions to each question booklet, underline any key words or phrases, such as *least, best, outline, describe,* and the like. In this way you will tend to answer as requested rather than discover on reviewing your paper that you *listed without describing,* that you selected the *worst* choice rather than the *best* choice, etc.

3. If the examination is of the objective or so-called multiple-choice type, that is, each question will also give a series of possible answers: A, B, C, or D, and you are called upon to select the best answer and write the letter next to that answer on your answer paper, it is advisable to start answering each question in turn. There may be anywhere from 50 to 100 such questions in the three or four hours allotted and you can see how much time would be taken if you read through all the questions before beginning to answer any. Furthermore, if you come across a question or a group of questions which you know would be difficult to answer, it would undoubtedly affect your handling of all the other questions.

4. If the examination is of the esssay-type and contains but a few questions, it is a moot point as to whether you should read all the questions before starting to answer any one. Of course if you are given a choice, say five out of seven and the like, then it is essential to read all the questions so you can eliminate the two which are most difficult. If, however, you are asked to answer all the questions, there may be danger in trying to answer the easiest one first because you may find that you will spend too much time on it. The best technique is to answer the first question, then proceed to the second, etc.

5. Time your answers. Before the examination begins, write down the time it started, then add the time allowed for the examination and write down the time it must be completed, then divide the time available somewhat as follows:

(a) If $3\frac{1}{2}$ hours are allowed, that would be 210 minutes. If you have 80 objective-type questions, that would be an average of $2\frac{1}{2}$ minutes per question. Allow yourself no more than 2 minutes per question, or a total of 160 minutes, which will permit about 50 minutes to review.

(b) If for the time allotment of 210 minutes, there are 7 essay questions to answer, that would average about 30 minutes a question. Give yourself only 25 minutes per question so that you have about 35 minutes to review.

6. The most important instruction is *to read each question* and make sure you know what is wanted. The second most important instruction is to *time yourself properly* so that you answer every question. The third most important instruction is to *answer every question*. Guess if you have to but include something for each question. Remember that you will receive no credit for a blank and will probably receive some credit if you write something in answer to an essay question. If you guess a letter, say "B" for a multiple-choice question, you may have guessed right. If you leave a blank as the answer to a multiple-choice question, the examiners may respect your feelings but it will not add a point to your score.

7. Suggestions
   a. <u>Objective-Type Questions</u>
   (1) Examine the question booklet for proper sequence of pages and questions.
   (2) Read all instructions carefully.
   (3) Skip any question which seems too difficult; return to it after all other questions have been answered.
   (4) Apportion your time properly; do not spend too much time on any single question or group of questions.
   (5) Note and underline key words -- *all, most, fewest, least, best, worst, same, opposite*.
   (6) Pay particular attention to negatives.
   (7) Note unusual option, e.g., unduly long, short, complex, different or similar in content to the body of the question.
   (8) Observe the use of "hedging" words -- *probably, may, most likely, etc.*
   (9) Make sure that your answer is put next to the same number as the question.
   (10) Do not second-guess unless you have good reason to believe the second answer is definitely more correct.
   (11) Cross out original answer if you decide another answer is more accurate; do not erase.
   (12) Answer all questions; guess unless instructed otherwise.
   (13) Leave time for review.
   b. <u>Essay-Type Questions</u>
   (1) Read each question carefully.
   (2) Determine exactly what is wanted. Underline key words or phrases.
   (3) Decide on outline or paragraph answer.
   (4) Include many different points and elements unless asked to develop any one or two points or elements.
   (5) Show impartiality by giving pros and cons unless directed to select one side only.
   (6) Make and write down any assumptions you find necessary to answer the question.
   (7) Watch your English, grammar, punctuation, choice of words.
   (8) Time your answers; don't crowd material.

8. Answering the Essay Question
   Most essay questions can be answered by framing the specific response around several key words or ideas. Here are a few such key words or ideas:

M's: manpower, materials, methods, money, management;
P's: purpose, program, policy, plan, procedure, practice, problems, pitfalls, personnel, public relations.

   a. <u>Six Basic Steps in Handling Problems</u>:
      (1) Preliminary plan and background development
      (2) Collect information, data and facts
      (3) Analyze and interpret information, data and facts
      (4) Analyze and develop solutions as well as make recommendations
      (5) Prepare report and sell recommendations
      (6) Install recommendations and follow up effectiveness
   b. <u>Pitfalls to Avoid</u>
      (1) *Taking things for granted*
         A statement of the situation does not necessarily imply that each of the elements is necessarily true; for example, a complaint may be invalid and biased so that all that can be taken for granted is that a complaint has been registered.
      (2) *Considering only one side of a situation*
         Wherever possible, indicate several alternatives and then point out the reasons you selected the best one.
      (3) *Failing to indicate follow-up*
         Whenever your answer indicates action on your part, make certain that you will take proper follow-up action to see how successful your recommendations, procedures, or actions turn out to be.
      (4) *Taking too long in answering any single question*
         Remember to time your answers properly.

IX. AFTER THE TEST

Scoring procedures differ in detail among civil service jurisdictions although the general principles are the same. Whether the papers are hand-scored or graded by the electric scoring machine we have described, they are nearly always graded by number. That is, the person who marks the paper knows only the number -- never the name -- of the applicant. Not until all the papers have been graded will they be matched with names. If other tests, such as training and experience or oral interview ratings have been given, scores will be combined. Different parts of the examination usually have different weights. For example, the written test might count 60 percent of the final grade, and a rating of training and experience 40 percent. In many jurisdictions, veterans will have a certain number of points added to their grades.

After the final grade has been determined, the names are placed in grade order and an eligible list is established. There are various methods for resolving ties between those who get the same final grade: probably the most common is to place first the name of the person whose application was received first. Job offers are made from the eligible list in the order the names appear on it.

You will be notified of your grade and your rank order as soon as all these computations have been made. This will be done as rapidly as possible.

People who are found to meet the requirements in the announcement are called "eligibles." Their names are put on a list of eligibles. An eligible's chances of getting a job depend on how high he stands on this list and how fast agencies are filling jobs from the list.

When a job is to be filled from a list of eligibles, the agency asks for the names of people on the list of eligibles for that job.

When the civil service commission receives this request, it sends to the agency the names of the three people highest on the list. Or, if the job to be filled has specialized requirements, the office sends the agency, from the general list, the names of the top three persons who meet those requirements.

The appointing officer makes a choice from among the three people whose names were sent to him. If the selected person accepts the appointment, the names of the others are put back on the list to be considered for future openings.

That is the rule in hiring from all kinds of eligible lists, whether they are for typist, carpenter, chemist, or something else. For every vacancy, the appointing officer has his choice of any one of the top three eligibles on the list. This explains why the person whose name is on top of the list sometimes does not get an appointment when some of the persons lower on the list do. If the appointing officer chooses the No.2 or No.3 eligible, the No.1 eligible does not get a job at once, but stays on the list until he is appointed or the list is terminated.

X. HOW TO PASS THE INTERVIEW TEST

The examination for which you applied requires an oral interview test. You have already taken the written test and you are now being called for the interview test -- the final part of the formal examination.

You may think that it is not possible to prepare for an interview test and that there are no procedures to follow during an interview.

Our purpose is to point out some things you can do in advance that will help you and some good rules to follow and pitfalls to avoid while you are being interviewed.

A. *WHAT IS AN INTERVIEW SUPPOSED TO TEST?*

The written examination is designed to test the technical knowledge and competence of the candidate; the oral is designed to evaluate intangible qualities, not readily measured otherwise, and to establish a list showing the relative fitness of each candidate, *as measured against his competitors,* for the position sought. Scoring is not on the basis of "right" or "wrong," but on a sliding scale of values ranging from "not passable" to "outstanding." As a matter of fact, it is possible to achieve a relatively low score without a single "incorrect" answer because of evident weakness in the qualities being measured.

Occasionally, an examination may consist entirely of an oral test -- either an individual or a group oral. In such cases, information is sought concerning the technical knowledges and abilities of the candidate, since there has been no written examination for this purpose. More commonly, however, an oral test is used to supplement a written examination.

B. *WHO CONDUCTS INTERVIEWS?*

The composition of oral boards varies among different jurisdictions. In nearly all, a representative of the personnel department serves as chairman. One of the members of the board may be a representative of the department in which the candidate would work. In some cases, "outside experts" are used, and, frequently, a business man or some other representative of the general public is asked to serve. Labor and management or other special groups may be represented. The aim is to secure the services of experts in the appropriate field.

However the board is composed, it is a good idea (and not at all improper or unethical) to ascertain in advance of the interview who the members are and what groups they represent. When you are introduced to them, you will have some idea of their backgrounds and interests, and at least you will not stutter and stammer over their names.

C. *WHAT TO DO BEFORE THE INTERVIEW*

While knowledge about the board members is useful and takes some of the surprise element out of the interview, there is other preparation which is more substantive. It *is* possible to prepare for an oral -- in several ways:

1. <u>Keep a Copy of Your Application and Review it Carefully Before the Interview</u>

    This may be the only document before the oral board, and the starting point of the interview. Know what experience and education you have listed there, and the sequence and dates of it. Sometimes the board will ask *you* to review the highlights of your experience for them; you should not have to hem and haw doing it.

2. <u>Study the Class Specification and the Examination Announcement</u>

    Usually, the oral board has one or both of these to guide them. The qualities, characteristics, or knowledges required by the position sought are stated in these documents. They offer valuable clues as to the nature of the oral interview. For example, if the job involves supervisory responsibilities, the announcement will usually indicate that knowledge of modern supervisory methods and the qualifications of the candidate as a supervisor will be tested. If so, you can expect such questions, frequently in the form of a hypothetical situation which you are expected to solve. *Never* go into an oral without knowledge of the duties and responsibilities of the job you seek.

3. <u>Think Through Each Qualification Required</u>

    Try to visualize the kind of questions *you* would ask if you were a board member. How well could you answer them? Try especially to appraise your own knowledge and background in each area, *measured against the job sought,* and identify any areas in which you are weak. Be critical and realistic -- do not flatter yourself.

4. <u>Do Some General Reading in Areas in Which You Feel You May be Weak</u>

    For example, if the job involves supervision and your past experience has *not,* some general reading in supervisory methods and practices, particularly in the field of human relations, might be useful. *Do not* study agency procedures or detailed manuals. The oral board will be testing your understanding and capacity, *not* your memory.

5. <u>Get a Good Night's Sleep and Watch Your General Health and Mental Attitude</u>

    You will want a clear head at the interview. Take care of a cold or other minor ailment, and, of course, *no hangovers*.

D. WHAT TO DO THE DAY OF THE INTERVIEW

Now comes the day of the interview itself. Give yourself plenty of time to get there. Plan to arrive somewhat ahead of the scheduled time, particularly if your appointment is in the fore part of the day. If a previous candidate fails to appear, the board might be ready for you a bit early. By early afternoon an oral board is almost invariably behind schedule if there are many candidates, and you may have to wait. Take along a book or magazine to read, or your application to review. But leave any extraneous material in the waiting room when you go in for your interview. In any event, relax and compose yourself.

The matter of dress is important. The board is forming impressions about you -- from your experience, your manners, your attitudes, and from your appearance. Give your personal appearance careful attention. Dress your *best*, but not your flashiest. Choose conservative, appropriate clothing, and be sure it and you are immaculate. This is a business interview, and your appearance should indicate that you regard it as such. Besides, being well-groomed and properly dressed will help boost your confidence.

Sooner or later, someone will call your name and escort you into the interview room. *This is it*. From here on you are on your own. It is too late for any more preparation. But, remember, you asked for this opportunity to prove your fitness, and you are here because your request was granted.

E. WHAT HAPPENS WHEN YOU GO IN?

The usual sequence of events will be as follows: The clerk (who is often the board stenographer) will introduce you to the chairman of the oral board, who will introduce you to each other member of the board. Acknowledge the introductions before you sit down. Do not be surprised if you find a microphone facing you or a stenotypist sitting by. Oral interviews are usually recorded, in the event of an appeal or other review.

Usually the chairman of the board will open the interview by reviewing the highlights of your education and work experience from your application -- primarily for the benefit of the other members of the board, as well as to get the material into the record. Do not interrupt or comment unless there is an error or significant misinterpretation; if so, do not hesitate. But do not quibble about insignificant matters. Usually, also, he will ask you some question about your education, your experience, or your present job -- partly to get you started talking, to establish the interviewing "rapport." He may start the actual questioning, or turn it over to one of the other members. Frequently each member undertakes the questioning on a particular area, one in which he is perhaps most competent. So you can expect each member to participate in the examination. And because the time is limited, you may expect some rather abrupt switches in the direction the questioning takes. Do not be upset by it. Normally, a board member will not pursue a single line of questioning unless he discovers a particular strength or weakness.

After each member has participated, the chairman will usually ask whether any member has any further questions, then will ask you if you have anything you wish to add. Unless you are expecting this question, it may floor you. Or worse, it may start you off on an extended, extemporaneous speech. The board is not usually seeking more information. The question is principally to offer you a last opportunity to present further qualifications or to indicate that you have nothing to add. So, if you feel that a significant qualification or characteristic has been overlooked, it is proper to point it out in a sentence or so. Do not compliment the board on the thoroughness of their examination -- they have been sketchy, and you know it. If you wish, merely say, "No thank you, I have nothing further to add." This is a point where you can "talk yourself out" of a good impression or fail to present an important bit of information. *Remember, you close the interview yourself.*

The chairman will then say,"That is all,Mr.Smith,thank you." Do not be startled; the interview is over, and quicker than you think. Say,"Thank you and good morning," gather up your belongings and take your leave. Save your sigh of relief for the other side of the door.

F. *HOW TO PUT YOUR BEST FOOT FORWARD*

Throughout all this process, you may feel that the board individually and collectively is trying to pierce your defenses, to seek out your hidden weaknesses, and to embarrass and confuse you. Actually, this is not true. They are obliged to make an appraisal of your qualifications for the job you are seeking, and they *want to see you in your best light*. Remember, they must interview all candidates and a noncooperative candidate may become a failure in spite of their best efforts to bring out his qualifications. Here are fifteen(15) suggestions that will help you:

1. <u>Be Natural. Keep Your Attitude Confident,But Not Cocky</u>

If *you* are not confident that you can do the job, do not exexpect the *board* to be. Do not apologize for your weaknesses, try to bring out your strong points. The board is interested in a positive, not a negative presentation. Cockiness will antagonize any board member, and make him wonder if you are covering up a weakness by a false show of strength.

2. <u>Get Comfortable, But Don't Lounge or Sprawl</u>

Sit erectly but not stiffly. A careless posture may lead the board to conclude you are careless in other things, or at least that you are not impressed by the importance of the occasion to you.Either conclusion is natural, even if incorrect. Do not fuss with your clothing, or with a pencil or an ashtray. Your hands may occasionally be useful to emphasize a point; do not let them become a point of distraction.

3. <u>Do Not Wisecrack or Make Small Talk</u>

This is a serious situation, and your attitude should show that you consider it as such. Further, the time of the board is limited; they do not want to waste it, and neither should you.

4. <u>Do Not Exaggerate Your Experience or Abilities</u>

In the first place, from information in the application,from other interviews and other sources, the board may know more about you than you think; in the second place, you probably will not get away with it in the first place. An experienced board is rather adept at spotting such a situation. Do not take the chance.

5. <u>If You Know a Member of the Board, Do Not Make a Point of It, Yet Do Not Hide It.</u>

Certainly you are not fooling him, and probably not the other members of the board. Do not try to take advantage of your acquaintanceship -- it will probably do you little good.

6. <u>Do Not Dominate the Interview</u>

Let the board do that. They will give you the clues -- do not assume that you have to do all the talking. Realize that the board has a number of questions to ask you, and do not try to take up all the interview time by showing off your extensive knowledge of the answer to the first one.

15

7. <u>Be Attentive</u>
You only have twenty minutes or so, and you should keep your attention at its sharpest throughout. When a member is addressing a problem or a question to you, give him your undivided attention. Address your reply principally to him, but do not exclude the other members of the board.
8. <u>Do Not Interrupt</u>
A board member may be stating a problem for you to analyze. He will ask you a question when the time comes. Let him state the problem, and wait for the question.
9. <u>Make Sure You Understand the Question</u>
Do not try to answer until you are sure what the question is. If it is not clear, restate it in your own words or ask the board member to clarify it for you. But do not haggle about minor elements.
10. <u>Reply Promptly But Not Hastily</u>
A common entry on oral board rating sheets is "candidate responded readily," or "candidate hesitated in replies." Respond as promptly and quickly as you can, but do not jump to a hasty, ill-considered answer.
11. <u>Do Not Be Peremptory in Your Answers</u>
A brief answer is proper -- but do not fire your answer back. That is a losing game from your point of view. The board member can probably ask questions much faster than you can answer them.
12. <u>Do Not Try To Create the Answer You Think the Board Member Wants</u>
He is interested in what kind of mind you have and how it works -- not in playing games. Furthermore, he can usually spot this practice and will usually grade you down on it.
13. <u>Do Not Switch Sides in Your Reply Merely to Agree With a Board Member</u>
Frequently, a member will take a contrary position merely to draw you out and to see if you are willing and able to defend your point of view. Do not start a debate, yet do not surrender a good position. If a position is worth taking, it is worth defending.
14. <u>Do Not Be Afraid to Admit an Error in Judgment if You Are Shown to Be Wrong</u>
The board knows that you are forced to reply without any opportunity for careful consideration. Your answer may be demonstrably wrong. If so, admit it and get on with the interview.
15. <u>Do Not Dwell at Length on Your Present Job</u>
The opening question may relate to your present assignment. Answer the question but do not go into an extended discussion. You are being examined for a *new* job, not your present one. As a matter of fact, try to phrase *all* your answers in terms of the job for which you are being examined.

G. *BASIS OF RATING*
Probably you will forget most of these "do's" and "don'ts" when you walk into the oral interview room. Even remembering them all will not insure you a passing grade. Perhaps you did not have the qualifications in the first place. But remembering them *will* help you to put your best foot forward, without treading on the toes of the board members.

Rumor and popular opinion to the contrary notwithstanding, an oral board wants you to make the best appearance possible. They know you are under pressure -- but they also want to see how you respond to it as a guide to what your reaction would be under the pressures of the job you seek. They will be influenced by the degree of poise you display, the **personal traits you show**, and the manner in which you respond.

EXAMINATION SECTION

EXAMINATION SECTION
TEST 1

DIRECTIONS: Each question or incomplete statement is followed by several suggested answers or completions. Select the one that BEST answers the question or completes the statement. *PRINT THE LETTER OF THE CORRECT ANSWER IN THE SPACE AT THE RIGHT.*

1. Which of the following types of seed will germinate under water?
   A. Bluegrass
   B. Red fescue
   C. Bentgrass
   D. Ryegrass

   1.___

2. Grass requires approximately _____ pounds of water for each pound of dry matter produced.
   A. 2   B. 80   C. 150   D. 500

   2.___

3. What is the term for a modified grass stem that grows aboveground and produces roots and new shoots at its joints?
   A. Stolon   B. Rhizome   C. Tuber   D. Stoma

   3.___

4. Ordinarily, the soil on the grounds of a golf course is likely to be deficient in one or more of the following elements EXCEPT
   A. phosphorus
   B. iron
   C. nitrogen
   D. potassium

   4.___

5. The main DISADVANTAGE associated with the use of warm season grasses is
   A. long winter dormancy periods
   B. low spread
   C. overseeding
   D. low leafspot resistance

   5.___

6. The use of water to help greens to hold a shot is generally not recommended; instead, where greens cannot be maintained properly to meet playing requirements, the recommended action is
   A. using gang rollers on the green
   B. mowing the green a little higher
   C. sloping up the edges slightly
   D. more frequent use of top-dressing

   6.___

7. Which of the following cool-season species has the poorest wear resistance?
   A. Kentucky bluegrass
   B. Red fescue
   C. Perennial ryegrass
   D. Creeping bentgrass

   7.___

8. In general, how many rounds are sustainable each year on a typical eighteen-hole golf course?
   A. 10,000-25,000
   B. 20,000-30,000
   C. 35,000-40,000
   D. 45,000-60,000

   8.___

9. During months of maximum play and turf growth, most putting greens are mowed daily at a height of ____ ". 9.___
    A. 1/32   B. 1/16   C. 1/8   D. 1/4

10. The summertime rate for hydrated lime application is typically ____ lbs. per 1,000 square feet. 10.___
    A. 5-10   B. 20-25   C. 30-40   D. 45-55

11. Which of the following elements serves to regulate the enzymatic processes of a plant? 11.___
    A. Phosphorus   B. Calcium
    C. Potassium   D. Nitrogen

12. Which of the following bluegrass cultivars has the greatest ability to survive poor nitrogen conditions? 12.___
    A. Delta   B. Merion   C. Glade   D. Wabash

13. When seedlings turn red and rot off at the ground line, the seed bed has become affected by 13.___
    A. earthworms   B. dollarspot
    C. damping-off fungus   D. grubs

14. Which of the following nitrogen sources has the greatest nitrogen content (%)? 14.___
    A. Activated sewage sludge   B. Urea
    C. Ammonium nitrate   D. Potassium nitrate

15. Before deciding how to treat soil, it is important to diagnose each of the following EXCEPT 15.___
    A. slope
    B. lime content
    C. soil reaction
    D. proportion of organic matter

16. In general, bentgrass nitrogen requirements can be determined by multiplying the number of growing months x ____ pounds of nitrogen per square feet. 16.___
    A. 1/4   B. 3/4   C. 1 to 1½   C. 2 to 3

17. Which of the following will *increase* the acidity of soil? 17.___
    A. Ammonium sulfate   B. Potassium nitrate
    C. Cyanamid   D. Muriate of phosphate

18. A turf manager's rule of thumb is that mowing is needed when the new extension of the leaves (the clippings) is approximately equal to 18.___
    A. one inch
    B. half the desired height of the cut
    C. the desired height of the cut
    D. the desired height of the cut, plus one inch

19. Of the following elements of a sprinkler irrigation system, which is generally LEAST important? The 19.___

A. topography of the land over which the system will operate
B. equipment used for distribution
C. water supply
D. capacity of the water transmission lines

20. As a general rule, it will take _____ pound(s) of sulfur to neutralize three pounds of calcium carbonate in soil.
    A. 1/2   B. 1   C. 3   D. 5

21. The LEAST effective time for weed control is usually
    A. late winter   B. late spring
    C. mid-summer   D. late fall

22. If seeding cannot be undertaken until after cold weather begins, it should be delayed until average temperatures have dropped below _____ °F.
    A. 15-20   B. 32   C. 35-40   D. 45-50

23. Which of the following is NOT a main factor in the calibration of a turfgrass sprayer?
    A. Nozzle spacing and length of boom
    B. Wind speed
    C. Discharge rate per nozzle
    D. Ground speed of sprayer

24. To support an eighteen-hole golf course, a clubhouse built to accommodate 600 members should occupy at least _____ square feet.
    A. 3000   B. 5000   C. 7000   D. 10,000

25. Which of the following species tends to have the shallowest root depth?
    A. Kentucky bluegrass   B. Bermudagrass
    C. Ryegrass   D. Bentgrass

KEY (CORRECT ANSWERS)

1. C
2. D
3. A
4. B
5. A

6. D
7. D
8. C
9. C
10. B

11. C
12. D
13. C
14. B
15. A

16. B
17. A
18. C
19. A
20. B

21. B
22. C
23. B
24. B
25. D

TEST 2

DIRECTIONS: Each question or incomplete statement is followed by several suggested answers or completions. Select the one that BEST answers the question or completes the statement. *PRINT THE LETTER OF THE CORRECT ANSWER IN THE SPACE AT THE RIGHT.*

1. To ensure a good flow of water through a course's drainage system, it is generally desirable to have the branches join the main at an angle of
   A. 15°   B. 40°   C. 60°   D. 90°

   1.___

2. Usually, about _____% of the quantity of nitrogen applied to turfgrass can be recovered in clippings during a growing season.
   A. 15   B. 35   C. 50   D. 80

   2.___

3. Of the following types of grasses, which is LEAST adapted for permanent turf golf courses in northern, cool, humid climes?
   A. Bentgrasses
   B. Ryegrasses
   C. Fescues
   D. Bluegrasses

   3.___

4. Calcium deficiency in grasses is indicated by
   A. yellowing blades
   B. stunted and curled new plant parts
   C. a scorched appearance along the margins of blades
   D. thinning spots

   4.___

5. Each of the following is a guideline/parameter for the installation of vertical trench and drain pipe EXCEPT
   A. using 0- to 30-foot spacing
   B. backfilling trenches to overflow with washed sand
   C. trenching 12-18" deep and 3" wide
   D. placing sod perpendicular to the trench

   5.___

6. If a green is built over gravelly or chalky soils, it is generally desirable to make up the surface with _____ inches of fertile soil.
   A. 2 to 4   B. 3 to 6   C. 9 to 12   D. 14 to 18

   6.___

7. Which of the following species generally has the BEST germination rate?
   A. Velvet bentgrass
   B. Rough bluegrass
   C. Red fescue
   D. Fairway wheatgrass

   7.___

8. When turf transpires water from leaf surfaces faster than the roots can absorb it from the soil, _____ occurs.
   A. photosynthesis
   B. wilting
   C. bracting
   D. saturation

   8.___

9. Which of the following is NOT a common mowing height for tees?
   A. 1/4"   B. 3/8"   C. 1/2"   D. 5/8"

10. Which of the following weeds is most likely to necessitate a total kill - with an agent such as glyphosate - for facilitating renovation?
    A. Chickweed
    B. Poa annua
    C. Tall fescue
    D. Nutsedge

11. Which of the following is NOT a benefit associated with the practice of deep turf piercing?
    A. Encouragement of deeper and more vigorous root growth
    B. Improved aggregation of mineral elements
    C. Facilitation of surface drainage during wet periods
    D. The even absorption of water and fertilizing elements

12. Of the following steps in preparing a turfgrass seedbed, which would be performed FIRST?
    A. Soil pulverizing, smoothing, and firming
    B. Loosening of soil to the required depth
    C. Incorporation of soil-texture-improving materials
    D. Sterilization for weed and insect control

13. Each of the following is a DISADVANTAGE associated with the practice of cool-season overseeding with ryegrasses EXCEPT
    A. may lose color in extreme cold
    B. competition with existing Bermuda
    C. dollarspot susceptibility
    D. slow growth

14. If a newly planted turf seedbed shows signs of crusting, the MOST likely cause is that
    A. the soil is too silty to support turf
    B. the period between water applications is too long
    C. a fungus has infested the topsoil
    D. too much water has been applied too fast

15. In what month, on a course in the northern United States, is nitrogen LEAST likely to be applied to turfgrass?
    A. March   B. August   C. November   D. January

16. Which of the following practices is MOST effective for the dispersal of worm casts?
    A. Brushing
    B. Verticutting
    C. Spiking
    D. Rolling

17. Which of the following chemicals would most likely be used to control an infestation of submerged aquatic weeds?
    A. Dalapron
    B. Aquathol
    C. Hydrothol
    D. 2,4-D

18. Grass blades that are rolled inward are described as
    A. hyaline   B. glabrous   C. involute   D. oblique

19. Which of the following is NOT an effect of lime on soils? It
    A. makes sandy soils more loamy in character
    B. causes clay and silt particles to form granulates
    C. increases the quantities of soluble iron and aluminum
    D. improves the supply of calcium and magnesium

20. If a bentgrass putting green is to be mowed at a height of 5/16", it should be verticut
    A. daily   B. weekly
    C. every two weeks   D. monthly

21. On a typical 18-hole course, about how much area (square feet) will be required for the storage of maintenance equipment?
    A. 1500   B. 3000   C. 7000   D. 10,000

22. The leaking of liquids from plant parts is known specifically as
    A. guttation   B. seepage
    C. leaching   D. adsorption

23. Which of the following species is not suitable for use on greens?
    A. Slender creeping red fescue
    B. Browntop bent
    C. Smooth-stalked meadow grass
    D. Chewings fescue

24. On a fairway, thatch depth can safely vary from about _____ inch.
    A. 1/16 to 1/8   B. 1/8 to 1/4
    C. 1/4 to 1/2   D. 1/2 to 1

25. If subsurface irrigation is to be used at all, it should be used on _____ soils.
    A. light   B. silty
    C. heavy   D. compacted clay

KEY (CORRECT ANSWERS)

1. B	6. C	11. B	16. A	21. B
2. C	7. A	12. B	17. B	22. A
3. B	8. B	13. D	18. C	23. C
4. B	9. D	14. D	19. C	24. C
5. D	10. C	15. C	20. D	25. A

EXAMINATION SECTION
TEST 1

DIRECTIONS: Each question or incomplete statement is followed by several suggested answers or completions. Select the one that BEST answers the question or completes the statement. *PRINT THE LETTER OF THE CORRECT ANSWER IN THE SPACE AT THE RIGHT.*

1. In regions where rainfall averages about 2-3 inches per month, leaching losses from the root zone of loam soil will amount to about _____ of the total water received.
    A. one-fourth
    B. one-half
    C. two-thirds
    D. the same amount

    1.___

2. Each of the following is a sign of potential manganese deficiency in grasses EXCEPT
    A. yellowing or striping between veins
    B. bent leaves
    C. curling or spotted leaves
    D. extreme stiffness

    2.___

3. Of the following substances, which is considered MOST desirable for *reducing* the alkaline reaction of soils?
    A. Sulfur   B. Gypsum   C. Ammonia   D. Lime

    3.___

4. For bluegrass, the standard seeding rate is about _____ pounds per 1,000 square feet.
    A. 2   B. 5   C. 8   D. 12

    4.___

5. In the northern regions, the MOST useful grasses for tees are
    A. Bermudagrasses
    B. bentgrasses
    C. zoysia
    D. redtop

    5.___

6. Generally, it is considered normal for an 18-hole golf course to have approximately _____ acres of fairway.
    A. 20-25   B. 30-40   C. 35-50   D. 40-60

    6.___

7. A course's turf manager is considering the use of zoysia. It will be important for him to know that its use would be appropriate for each of the following EXCEPT
    A. on fairways
    B. around sand traps
    C. on south and west slopes
    D. on shaded tees

    7.___

8. Generally, the discharge of a sprinkler head will increase by about ____% if the pressure is doubled.
    A. 40   B. 50   C. 75   D. 100

    8.___

9. The use of mole drains is generally limited to
    A. types of soils in which the channels will remain open for a reasonable time
    B. elevated structures such as tees
    C. areas with active percolation
    D. areas with limited channel outlets

10. Each of the following is a DISADVANTAGE associated with using effluent water for a golf course irrigation EXCEPT
    A. higher corrosion
    B. high salt content
    C. excessive *dryness* of water
    D. potential iron chlorosis

11. Which of the following elements provides grasses with a mechanism for using and transforming energy?
    A. Nitrogen
    B. Magnesium
    C. Phosphorus
    D. Potassium

12. Generally, _____ weeks of favorable weather are needed for recovery of turfgrass following severe renovation.
    A. 2   B. 4   C. 6   D. 10

13. The daily consumption of water by turf varies widely according to a number of factors, but it can comfortably be estimated at between _____ gal. per 1,000 square feet.
    A. 1-5   B. 5-35   C. 10-60   D. 75-100

14. Tees should be watered
    A. every four hours
    B. twice weekly
    C. at periods that allow the shortest possible time between applications
    D. at periods that allow the longest possible time between applications

15. The MOST advantageous time for coring warm season grass turf is during
    A. late winter
    B. early summer
    C. late fall
    D. late summer

16. To facilitate surface water runoff on a course, all surfaces must involve a fall of not less than 1 in
    A. 12   B. 55   C. 100   D. 170

17. A turf manager's rule of thumb is that during any one mowing, no more than _____ of the green tissue of the turf should be removed.
    A. 1/8   B. 1/3   C. 1/2   D. 3/4

18. What is the term for any component of a pesticide mixture that modifies the mixture beneficially?
    A. Protectant
    B. Surfactant
    C. Adjuvant
    D. Filler

19. One cubic yard of sand topdressing is applied to 5,000 square feet of turf. Approximately what is the thickness, in inches, of the topdressing layer?
    A. 1/32   B. 1/16   C. 1/8   D. 1/4

    19.___

20. A golf course's manual sprinkler insert system uses a pipe diameter of 3 inches, and extends for a total pipe length of 10,000 feet. Approximately how many tee and green valves will be needed for the system?
    A. 12-18   B. 30-40   C. 95   D. 150

    20.___

21. Each of the following is an advantage associated with the use of organic nitrogen compounds on turfgrass EXCEPT
    A. lower leaching losses
    B. easier handling
    C. relatively higher water solubility
    D. less danger of burning

    21.___

22. An ideal clay loam rootzone would contain about ____% air, subject to water variations.
    A. 10   B. 25   C. 40   D. 50

    22.___

23. Drainage ditches on the course should not allow a water fall velocity of greater than 3 feet per second, or a fall of ____ ft. per mile, in order to avoid bank cutting.
    A. ½ to 1   B. 1 to 2½ C. 3½ to 7 D. 6 to 10

    23.___

24. Which of the following is NOT a symptom of zinc deficiency in a grass?
    A. Witch's brooms
    B. Yellowing and bronzing of stunted leaves
    C. Intravenal yellowing
    D. Dark, thin, desiccating leaves that turn white in advanced stages

    24.___

25. Mulch should be removed from a turf seeding when grass seedlings have grown ____ inch(es).
    A. ¼   B. ½ to 1   C. 3/4 to 1½ D. 1 to 2

    25.___

KEY (CORRECT ANSWERS)

1. A	6. B	11. C	16. C	21. C
2. D	7. D	12. B	17. B	22. B
3. A	8. A	13. C	18. C	23. A
4. A	9. A	14. D	19. B	24. C
5. B	10. C	15. B	20. C	25. B

TEST 2

DIRECTIONS: Each question or incomplete statement is followed by several suggested answers or completions. Select the one that BEST answers the question or completes the statement. *PRINT THE LETTER OF THE CORRECT ANSWER IN THE SPACE AT THE RIGHT.*

1. The last two nozzle numbers printed on a turfgrass sprayer nozzle indicate the
   A. gallons per minute of spray that can be applied at 40 PSI
   B. recommended ground speed of the sprayer
   C. volume in quarts of spray that can be applied for every acre covered
   D. angle of the spray discharge

1.___

2. Throughout the southern region, _____ and centipedegrass generally have the widest adaptations for fairway use.
   A. fescue   B. colonial bentgrass
   C. Bermudagrass   D. bluegrass

2.___

3. Which of the following chemicals would LEAST likely be used to control an infestation of algae?
   A. Cutrine plus   B. Hydrothol
   C. Aquathol   D. Copper sulfate

3.___

4. As a means of irrigation, surface flooding is used in limited instances, and usually on
   A. fairways   B. tees
   C. greens   D. approaches

4.___

5. Golf courses generally need a water supply that will provide approximately _____ gallons per minute for nine holes.
   A. 100   B. 250   C. 500   D. 1000

5.___

6. Which of the following will *decrease* the acidity of soil?
   A. Calcium nitrate   B. Ureaform
   C. Activated sewage sludge   D. Urea

6.___

7. _____ pounds is the recommended rate for overseeding ryegrass for a 1,000 square foot area.
   A. 3-8   B. 10-15   C. 20-30   D. 40-60

7.___

8. Which of the following is NOT an inorganic nitrogen compound used on turf?
   A. Ammonium nitrate   B. Ammonium sulfate
   C. Arsenic   D. Urea

8.___

9. In general, which areas of a golf course are most prone to infestations of Poa annua?
   A. Tees
   B. Greens
   C. Aprons and collars
   D. Fairways

10. Generally, the BEST months in which to undertake the renovation of unsatisfactory putting greens are
    A. December and January
    B. March and April
    C. June and July
    D. August and September

11. Regardless of the germination rate advertised, for turfgrass in the field the rate is normally around ____%.
    A. 10   B. 30   C. 50   D. 75

12. The soil on a course requires between 3/4 and 1 inch of water to satisfy its capillary capacity to a 6-inch depth. This soil would MOST likely be characterized as
    A. loamy   B. silty   C. clumpy   D. sandy

13. Which of the following is NOT typically controlled by the annual application of herbicides?
    A. Crabgrass
    B. Knotweed
    C. Wild garlic
    D. Poa annua

14. Ordinarily, if a full amount of needed lime is applied to a course in a single dose, the requirement is about _____ pounds of crushed limestone per acre.
    A. 500   B. 1,000   C. 2,000   D. 3,000

15. Which of the following warm-season species has the poorest wear resistance?
    A. Carpetgrass
    B. Zoysia
    C. Bermuda
    D. Bahia

16. Though a part of the area assigned to a putting green is expected to be taken up by the surrounds, at LEAST ____% should be available for placing the hole if a green is to be used to an extent commensurate with its size.
    A. 50   B. 70   C. 85   D. 95

17. Which of the following nitrogen sources has the greatest tendency to absorb moisture?
    A. Ammonium sulfate
    B. Ammonium nitrate
    C. Potassium nitrate
    D. Ureaformaldehyde

18. When grass is growing vigorously and the weather is hot and dry, the losses in moisture will average from ½ to 1 inch of water every
    A. 12 to 24 hours
    B. 24 to 48 hours
    C. 2 to 4 days
    D. 5 to 7 days

19. Which of the following species generally has the greatest purity for its cleaned seed?
    A. Ryegrass
    B. Blue grama
    C. Redtop
    D. Fairway wheatgrass

20. The most satisfactory way of adapting watering to the needs of various grasses on a golf course is by adjusting the
    A. water pressure
    B. area to be watered at one time
    C. total time of an application
    D. time between applications

21. In general, the proliferation of weeds is encouraged by _____ soils.
    A. acidic   B. silty   C. alkaline   D. gravelly

22. The application of inorganic nitrogen compounds to turf-grass may cause excessive stimulation. Generally, a rate of _____ lb(s). of actual nitrogen per 1,000 square feet of turf is considered to be the upper limit.
    A. 1/4 to 3/4
    B. 1 to 1½
    C. 2 to 4
    D. 3½ to 5

23. Each of the following is an advantage associated with the practice of cool-season overseeding with creeping red fescue EXCEPT
    A. good putting
    B. long-lived
    C. extreme disease resistance
    D. less frequent mowing

24. When the lift required of a sprinkler system is less than 15 feet, it is customary to use _____ pumps.
    A. centrifugal
    B. turbine
    C. vacuum
    D. displacement

25. Each of the following is a condition necessary for soil denitrification EXCEPT
    A. denitrifying organism
    B. presence of nitrates
    C. existing energy source
    D. high levels of oxygen

KEY (CORRECT ANSWERS)

1. A	6. A	11. B	16. B	21. C
2. C	7. D	12. D	17. B	22. B
3. C	8. C	13. C	18. C	23. B
4. A	9. C	14. C	19. A	24. A
5. C	10. D	15. A	20. D	25. D

EXAMINATION SECTION
TEST 1

DIRECTIONS: Each question or incomplete statement is followed by several suggested answers or completions. Select the one that BEST answers the question or completes the statement. *PRINT THE LETTER OF THE CORRECT ANSWER IN THE SPACE AT THE RIGHT.*

1. Assume that the ticket agent at the bathhouse cannot dispense tickets from his machine because of a mechanical failure.
   You should authorize the ticket agent to
   A. sell tickets by hand from the bundle only
   B. stop selling tickets and await the installation of a stand-by machine
   C. collect cash from the patrons and have them escorted through the bathhouse entrance gate
   D. let the patrons deposit admission fees in a box at the bathhouse entrance gate

   1.___

2. If an operator of a four-wheel drive beach buggy leaves the sand portion of a beach and neglects to disengage his forward gears when he starts to drive over area streets to the dump or drop area, he will
   A. cause his transmission to lose linkage
   B. excessively wear his emergency brake
   C. jam up his front differential
   D. seriously damage the springs of the vehicle

   2.___

3. Inventories and replacement of material, supplies, and equipment required for pre-season preparation of beaches is normally scheduled to begin immediately after
   A. April 1st   B. Memorial Day
   C. Labor Day   D. New Year's Day

   3.___

4. On an Emerson Resuscitator, the cylinder is considered full when the cylinder volume indicator shows AT LEAST _____ lbs. pressure per square inch or more.
   A. 900   B. 1300   C. 1800   D. 2800

   4.___

5. The term *deadman*, when used in training courses for lifeguards assigned to oceanfront beaches, refers to
   A. a rope splicing tool
   B. beach cradles
   C. upland anchorage
   D. a fixed warning sign on a stone jetty

   5.___

6. The appropriate arm signal for a lifeguard to give from a standing position on his tower to call for delivery of a resuscitator is:
   A. Pump one arm up and down from an overhead position
   B. Rotary motion in front of chest
   C. Arms extended up -- straight overhead
   D. Arms clasped overhead

   6.___

7. The standard technique for executing the back pressure - arm lift method of artificial respiration requires the operator to adhere to a cycle consisting of a prescribed series of motions.
This cycle should be repeated about _____ times per minute.
   A. two   B. four   C. six   D. twelve

8. Assume that an elderly swimmer has collapsed while swimming. His friend, who is with him, states that the victim has a long history of heart failure. The victim is brought to the first aid station showing signs of shock and labored breathing.
You should take which one of the following actions?
   A. Apply an oxygen mask tightly to the victim's face
   B. Using the resuscitator, turn on the inhalator valve and apply the face mask
   C. Get him dressed and send him to a hospital with his friend
   D. Wrap him in blankets to keep warm and give him a hot beverage

9. The symptoms of heat prostration MOST usually are:
   A. Face pale, pulse weak; perspiration profuse on forehead, face, and hands; faintness and nausea
   B. Face red, hot, and dry; pulse strong and fast, high fever; perhaps nausea
   C. Face purplish; pulse erratic; feet and hands cold
   D. Face pale; respiration rate down to six; patient violent

10. Of the following, the BEST method for controlling algae growth in outdoor swimming pools is to
    A. treat with heavy dosages of chlorine
    B. raise the pH with additional amounts of calcium carbonate
    C. apply standard rates of copper sulphate
    D. lower the pool level and add fresh water from the main

11. To improve the capabilities of swimming pool filters, a jelly-like substance called a *flock* must be deposited on the surface of the filter bed.
The flock is formed by adding which of the following two chemicals to the water in the treatment tank?
    A. Anhydrous ammonia and sodium dichromate
    B. Aluminum sulphate and sodium carbonate
    C. Orthotolidine and copper sulphate
    D. Iodides and calcium chloride

12. Pool water returning from the center drain of an outdoor swimming pool is called the
    A. confluent   B. effluent   C. influent   D. affluent

13. Backwashing in a conventional water treatment plant is USUALLY performed by the plant operator when the loss of head reaches _____ pounds per square inch.
    A. 3½-4   B. 5½-7   C. 8-10   D. 11-12

14. Most outdoor swimming pool operations have large heating boilers. These boilers have water columns with look-through water gauges, showing the water level in the boiler. The manual on maintenance and operation of heating plants and auxiliary equipment specifies that, while the boiler is in operation, the water column and gauge glass should be blown down
    A. daily   B. weekly   C. bi-weekly   D. monthly

15. Conventional gun-type oil burners used at park facilities are required to utilize as fuel
    A. #2 oil
    B. #4 oil
    C. #6 oil
    D. a kerosene mixture

16. Chlorine residual in municipally operated pools as required by the department of health shall be kept at NOT LESS THAN _____ ppm.
    A. 0.01   B. 0.25   C. 0.45   D. 1.0

17. Which of the following should be used to test the pH range (alkaline range) of swimming pool water?
    A. Ultraviolet light
    B. Iodides
    C. Orthotolodine
    D. Bromo-thymol blue

18. The filtration rate per square foot for a conventional filter is _____ gallons per square foot.
    A. 8   B. 6   C. 5   D. 3

19. Chlorine gas in steel cylinders is used as a sterilant in most outdoor swimming pools.
    If chlorine gas leaks occur from faulty connections, valve packings, etc., the STANDARD procedure for locating the leaks promptly is to use
    A. a lighted sulphur taper
    B. a soapy mixture
    C. acetone, applied with a camel hair brush
    D. concentrated ammonia

20. The MOST desirable time to apply lime to fairways on a golf course that is high in the acid range is
    A. during the rainy season   B. after a long, dry spell
    C. in the fall or spring   D. in late January

21. A bag of commercial fertilizer with a 10-6-4 classification on the printed face of the bag contains which of the following combination of chemicals by weight?
    A. 10% phosphoric acid, 6% nitrogen, and 4% potash
    B. 10% potash, 6% phosphoric acid, and 4% nitrogen
    C. 10% nitrogen, 6% phosphoric acid, and 4% potash
    D. 10% potash, 6% nitrogen, and 4% phosphoric acid

22. The turf on a tee with 15,000 square feet is badly worn because of traffic density and must be completely rehabilitated. You have completed the step requiring the application of a soil sterilant, and you are ready to apply nitrogen to the soil at a rate of two pounds of available nitrogen per thousand square feet.
How many 100 pound bags of 10-6-4 fertilizer must be applied to adequately supply the nitrogen requirements?
   A. 10 B. 8 C. 5 D. 3

23. According to regulations relating to lawn-making, which of the following pH ratings of fertilizer is desirable?
   A. 4.5 to 5.0
   B. 5.5 to 6.0
   C. 6.5 to 7.0
   D. 7.5 to 8.0

24. To facilitate photosynthesis for normal growth, grass should be mowed often enough so that clippings are
   A. equal to mowing height
   B. shorter than mowing height
   C. longer than mowing height
   D. two inches long

25. Of the following, the MOST suitable grass seed mixture for a play field is one containing Kentucky bluegrass and
   A. colonial bent
   B. Bermuda grass
   C. zoysia
   D. creeping red fescue

26. Red fescue is USUALLY added to a seed mixture because of its
   A. drought resistance
   B. fast germination
   C. slow germination
   D. coarse texture

27. The four basic procedures generally considered as constituting the minimum maintenance for turf are: (1) selection of adapted grasses; (2) fertilization; (3) watering; and (4)
   A. aerification
   B. mowing
   C. plugging
   D. rolling

28. The BEST method for improving the soil structure of a heavily compacted playfield is to apply organic topdressing first and then proceed with
   A. pesticide application
   B. mowing and watering
   C. fertilization
   D. aerification

29. A fairway should be maintained so that its width averages _____ to _____ feet.
   A. 60; 110 B. 120; 210 C. 220; 260 D. 270; 310

30. A good supplemental program to aid the grass that is already growing and to establish new grass in the thin, worn-out areas of an athletic field is
   A. overseeding
   B. rolling
   C. plugging
   D. watering

KEY (CORRECT ANSWERS)

1. A	11. B	21. C
2. C	12. B	22. D
3. C	13. B	23. C
4. C	14. A	24. B
5. C	15. A	25. D
6. C	16. D	26. A
7. D	17. D	27. B
8. B	18. D	28. D
9. A	19. D	29. B
10. C	20. C	30. A

TEST 2

DIRECTIONS: Each question or incomplete statement is followed by several suggested answers or completions. Select the one that BEST answers the question or completes the statement. *PRINT THE LETTER OF THE CORRECT ANSWER IN THE SPACE AT THE RIGHT.*

1. Traps are CUSTOMARILY surfaced with a layer of sand about _____ inches deep.
   A. 6   B. 12   C. 18   D. 24

2. A GOOD medium sandy loam for a putting green should contain _____ organic content.
   A. 5-10%   B. 10-15%   C. 20-30%   D. 30-50%

3. In the maintenance of a putting green, the LEAST necessary piece of equipment is
   A. putting green mower B. power sprayer
   C. aerator   D. fertilizer spreader

4. The BEST way to maintain a green so that it holds a pitched ball is by
   A. overwatering   B. good soil structure
   C. underwatering   D. high mowing

5. The surface soil on a green should be a medium sandy loam placed _____ to _____ inches deep.
   A. 2; 4   B. 4; 6   C. 8; 10   D. 12; 18

6. The BEST turf fertilizers today contain about
   A. 85% slow-release phosphorus
   B. 16% fast-release nitrogen
   C. 50% slow-release nitrogen
   D. 20% phosphorus

7. Since golf course grasses are heavy users of phosphorus, potassium, magnesium, and calcium, the BEST pH range for turf, where maximum quantities of these chemicals are available, is
   A. 4.2 to 4.8   B. 5.0 to 5.8
   C. 6.0 to 7.0   D. 7.2 to 8.2

8. Damage on golf greens and other turf areas caused by the *Fusarium nivale* fungus (snow mold) can BEST be prevented or adequately checked by treatment with
   A. ammonium methyl arsenates
   B. aluminum sulphate
   C. hydrated lime
   D. cadminates

9. To prevent snow mold, treatment should GENERALLY start   9.___
   A. in early spring   B. after a heavy rain
   C. in late winter   D. after a heavy snow

10. Chlordane is used in turf management to   10.___
    A. eradicate goose grass   B. control brown patch
    C. grub-proof soil   D. stimulate root growth

11. Artificial rinks have refrigerants to cool the brine   11.___
    which is constantly circulated through the wrought-iron
    pipes imbedded in the floor of the rink.
    The brine can be chilled to below zero degrees Fahrenheit
    because it contains a chemical salt known as
    A. sodium chloride   B. calcium chloride
    C. calcium carbonate   D. ammonium chloride

12. The MINIMUM ice thickness generally considered safe for   12.___
    ice skating on a lake or pond whose depth does not exceed
    3 feet is _____ inches.
    A. 2   B. 3   C. 5   D. 6

13. In the operation of an ice skating rink, prior to start-   13.___
    ing the process of ice building, the slab surface should
    be painted with _____ paint.
    A. white water   B. white epoxy
    C. blue water   D. blue epoxy

14. Crowd control in an ice skating rink includes all phases   14.___
    of the patrons' activities from admissions line-up to the
    time the patrons leave the rink.
    According to regulations, during special sessions, guards
    should
    A. skate in a clockwise direction
    B. skate in a counterclockwise direction
    C. be positioned on the ice near the entrances
    D. be positioned off the ice near the entrances

15. When a rink slab has been chilled below freezing tempera-   15.___
    ture, ice can be built to the desired thickness by spray-
    ing a fine layer of water onto the slab with a
    A. Toro sprayer   B. Skinner sprinkler
    C. Rainboni   D. Zamboni

16. The following is a description of the cooling system of a   16.___
    skating rink: The refrigerant (ammonia or freon) absorbs
    the heat from the circulating brine which, in turn, lowers
    the temperature of the skating slab; when the brine is
    returned to the chiller after leaving the rink floor with
    absorbed heat, the compressor pumps the refrigerant gases
    to the condenser.
    The condenser does which of the following?
    It
    A. cools the refrigerant gas to a liquid and returns it
       to the chiller
    B. heats up the refrigerant gas
    C. transforms the gas into ice crystals
    D. cools the circulating water within the condenser

17. At indoor rinks where atmospheric temperatures remain stable and are not affected by outdoor weather conditions, brine should be circulated at a temperature of APPROXIMATELY _____ degrees Fahrenheit.
    A. 7   B. 10   C. 15   D. 25

18. Conditioning ice surfaces on outdoor rinks in early fall or late spring is BEST accomplished
    A. after each session   B. after the sun sets
    C. at 8 A.M.   D. at 12 noon

19. The standard of thickness for safe skating on lakes and ponds with water depths over three feet is _____ inches.
    A. two   B. three   C. five   D. seven

20. Assume that a heavy snowstorm has reached the area at the start of the evening session of outdoor rink operations. The one of the following actions that should be taken is to
    A. send all the skaters home, telling them the rink is closed
    B. let them skate until the snow is too deep to move
    C. cone off one-half of the rink at a time for snow removal operations
    D. give snow shovels to as many skaters as possible and put them to work clearing the rink

21. Of the following trees, the one which is NOT recommended for street tree planting is
    A. London plane   B. Gingko
    C. Yellow Pine   D. Pin Oak

22. Before useful measures can be applied to control a tree disease epidemic in a park, it is FIRST necessary to
    A. obtain an appropriation for spraying
    B. have a correct diagnosis made of the disease
    C. make an inventory of the diseased trees
    D. wait until winter when the trees are dormant

23. Of the following trees, the one which is generally MOST often recommended for sandy soils is
    A. American elm   B. Japanese maple
    C. Chinese poplar   D. Japanese black pine

24. About 75 percent of all tree diseases, including all mildews, rusts, anthracnoses, and sooty molds, are caused by
    A. fungi   B. viruses   C. nematodes   D. bacteria

25. Tree crews should be instructed to ALWAYS
    A. trim the leader of a tree to improve its vitality
    B. prune trees by removing at least 50% of the crowns
    C. remove all injured and diseased wood
    D. fertilize a tree before pruning it

26. Three techniques that you can use to evaluate maintenance activities and determine whether they can be done better are work simplification, work measurement, and
    A. establishment of work performance standards
    B. use of labor saving devices
    C. increased supervision
    D. computerization

27. Staffing is BEST indicated by which of the following activities?
    A. Selection and training of personnel and maintaining favorable conditions of work
    B. Structuring an organization for unity of command, span of control, and lines of authority
    C. Writing task lists for the different titles working at a facility
    D. Working out in broad outline the things that need to be done and the methods for doing them to accomplish the mission of the agency

28. Generally, the MOST practical way to ascertain most readily the number of man-hours it takes to do a job is by
    A. referring to a management analysis handbook
    B. making a detailed analysis of the job
    C. asking the operator performing the job
    D. reviewing job specifications

29. Any violation of the rules or regulations for the government and protection of public parks and property shall be punishable by NOT MORE THAN _____ imprisonment or by a fine of not more than _____ dollars, or by both.
    A. thirty days'; fifty
    B. sixty days'; one hundred
    C. ninety days'; two hundred fifty
    D. one year's; five hundred

30. One workman can hand-rake leaves at the rate of approximately 1,000 square feet in 20 minutes.
    How many men would you assign to a crew to hand rake a grove of trees covering 40,000 square feet in order to accomplish the job within three hours?
    A. 3   B. 30   C. 50   D. 5

KEY (CORRECT ANSWERS)

1. A	6. C	11. B	16. A	21. C	26. A
2. C	7. C	12. B	17. C	22. B	27. A
3. B	8. D	13. A	18. A	23. D	28. C
4. B	9. A	14. D	19. C	24. A	29. A
5. C	10. C	15. D	20. C	25. C	30. D

EXAMINATION SECTION
TEST 1

DIRECTIONS: Each question or incomplete statement is followed by several suggested answers or completions. Select the one that BEST answers the question or completes the statement. *PRINT THE LETTER OF THE CORRECT ANSWER IN THE SPACE AT THE RIGHT.*

1. To cut a number of 2" x 4" lengths of wood accurately at an angle of 45°, it is BEST to use a
   A. coping saw
   B. mitre-box
   C. square
   D. marking gauge

2. The leverage that can be obtained with a wrench is determined MAINLY by the
   A. material of which the wrench is made
   B. gripping surface of the jaw
   C. length of the handle
   D. thickness of the wrench

3. Many electric power tools, such as drills, have a third conductor in the line cord which should be connected to a grounded part of the power receptacle.
   The reason for this is to
   A. have a spare wire in case one power wire should break
   B. strengthen the power lead so that it cannot be easily damaged
   C. protect the user of the tool from electric shocks
   D. allow use of the tool for extended periods of time without overheating

4. A cold chisel whose head has become *mushroomed* should NOT be used primarily because
   A. it is impossible to hit the head squarely
   B. the chisel will not cut accurately
   C. chips might fly from the head
   D. the chisel has lost its *temper*

5. Catch basins are used in connection with
   A. buried gas mains
   B. underground springs
   C. storm water sewer systems
   D. water heaters

6. The ratio of air to gasoline in an automobile engine is controlled by the
   A. gas filter
   B. fuel pump
   C. carburetor
   D. distributor

7. Which of the following trees recommended for street planting has been greatly overused?
   A. London Plane
   B. Flowering Japanese Cherry
   C. Dawn Redwood
   D. Red Oak

8. Generally, during dry weather, a clay tennis court should be
    A. wet down at the end of each day's play, then well rolled early the next morning
    B. well rolled at the end of each day's play, then wet down early the next morning
    C. wet down and well rolled at the end of each day's play
    D. wet down and well rolled early each morning before play

9. The playing surface of a clay tennis court *generally* consists of
    A. silt
    B. clay, silt, and sand
    C. clay and silt
    D. silt and sand

10. Of the following, the frequency with which revenues from beaches, swimming pools, golf courses, and ice skating rinks are *normally* prepared for deposit is
    A. twice daily
    B. daily
    C. twice a week
    D. weekly

11. The one of the following which is the BEST time, as a general rule, for removing debris deposited on the beaches by the tide during the winter is
    A. every day
    B. once a week
    C. once a month
    D. only before the opening of the beaches for the summer

12. Snow fences are usually used at beaches in winter PRIMARILY to
    A. prevent snow from drifting too high near buildings
    B. prevent driftwood from coming too far up on the beaches
    C. control wind erosion of sand from the beaches
    D. temporarily replace regular fences and railings which are damaged

13. Of the following, the filter material used in all of the gravity system filters of public swimming pools is
    A. sand
    B. diatomaceous earth
    C. anthrafilt
    D. resin-impregnated paper

14. At an outdoor public rink, the PROPER procedure during a snowfall *normally* is to
    A. close half the rink at a time for snow removal, leaving the other half open for skating
    B. disregard the snow until the normal end of sessions, at which time snow should be removed and ice renovated
    C. close the rink, as snow usually creates hazardous skating conditions
    D. clear the rink, then melt the snow with a hot-water spray; skating may be resumed when the water freezes

15. If ice expands or contracts because of temperature fluctuations, large fissures or cracks can form. Such cracks *generally* are
    A. *abnormal* and an indication of thin ice conditions
    B. *normal*, but can become trip hazards, and so should be filled in
    C. *normal* and safe, and can be ignored
    D. *very common*, and the best indication of thin ice

16. According to instructions, the FIRST and MOST important duty performed each morning by every greensman at a golf course is to _____ the greens.
    A. water   B. mow   C. rake   D. whip

17. A golfer is entitled to tee off and must be ready to tee off when his number is called by the starter.
    Golfers not present or ready to tee off when their number is called will, upon returning to the starter's board, be reassigned by the starter _____ numbers below the number _____.
    A. 10; on their ticket
    B. 10; being called at the time of their return
    C. 20; on their ticket
    D. 20; being called at the time of their return

18. Assume that a player is at a public golf course which is not a pitch-putt course, and that this golfer does not have an approved adjustable club.
    Of the following, the equipment that this player MUST have is
    A. at least three golf clubs, including a putter and one wood
    B. at least seven golf clubs, including a putter and one wood
    C. a golf bag or carrier and at least three golf clubs, one of which must be a putter
    D. a golf bar or carrier and at least seven golf clubs, including a putter and one wood

19. Ball marks on golf course greens must be repaired as they occur.
    To repair such marks before they dry out, each greensman must be equipped with a
    A. sharp table fork or penknife
    B. bamboo or wooden rake
    C. spade
    D. watering can

20. Performance of necessary maintenance on machines according to a regular schedule is generally
    A. *desirable*, primarily because the appearance of machinery should be kept up
    B. *undesirable*, primarily because it is a waste of both man-hours and machine-hours to repair functioning machinery

    C. *undesirable*, primarily because too much maintenance is as bad as not enough
    D. *desirable*, primarily because regularly maintained machinery is more efficient and less likely to suffer a major breakdown at a time when it is urgently needed

21. During your regular inspection tour, you notice a youth writing on a statue.
Of the following, the BEST immediate action for long-range results is for you to
    A. ignore the youth, because if you indicate to him that he is wrong, he will only continue to write
    B. approach the youth and inform him that you will take him to police headquarters for breaking park department rules
    C. tell the youth that you know he has defaced property throughout the park and is prohibited by law from entering the park again
    D. talk to the youth concerning the cost of graffiti, give him a sincere but stern warning on the penalties involved, and suggest that he join a *neighborhood task force*

22. An irate citizen telephones you to state her anger about a parks department employee. She states that the employee has asked her children not to pick shrubs or flowers and the children were heartbroken because they were making a bouquet for their grandmother. The mother states that the park is for the enjoyment of the public and such action by the employee was unwarranted.
Of the following, the BEST method of handling the situation is for you to
    A. apologize for the employee by informing the citizen that he was new and did not understand children
    B. inform the caller that she will have to file a written complaint to the parks department
    C. sympathize with the caller, but tell her that park rules prohibit such action because it marks the beauty of the park
    D. tell the caller that park employees are properly trained, and always perform correctly

23. After repeated warnings by you about violation of parks department regulations, two concessionaries have had their permits revoked. The two wish to be reinstated and have asked local community groups to intervene. The groups, concerned with protecting the rights of the citizens against unwarranted actions, have come to you asking for the reasons for the revocations and for all information related to them.
Of the following, the BEST course of action for you to take for the maintenance of good public relations is to

A. state that information concerning internal operations is confidential
B. provide the information requested, avoiding opinions and off-the-record comments
C. inform the groups that you do not know the reasons for the permit revocations, but you will inform them as soon as the information becomes available
D. explain that standards are set for concessionaires and any departure from these regulations is cause for revocation

24. Assume that as a newly appointed supervisor, one of the first work orders you issue involves painting and restoring equipment in a little-used children's play area in a district park.
The one of the following which would be the MOST likely effect upon patrons who frequent such areas is that this would
    A. create better public relations, since a pleasing appearance of physical facilities helps establish confidence in the park system
    B. have no effect on public relations since the area was not often used
    C. create poor public relations since such repairs will require closing the area
    D. raise suspicions concerning the park's efficiency, since it was senseless to improve a little-used play area

25. In order to get maximum use of facilities adjacent to an outdoor pool, you have decided to open the pavilions as winter recreation centers for indoor games.
Of the following, the MOST important factor for the effectiveness of such a program is generally
    A. how well the immediate director is known and liked
    B. the amount of publicity news media give the program
    C. how well similar park programs have been accepted by the public
    D. how well the public understands and cooperates with the program

KEY (CORRECT ANSWERS)

1. B	6. C	11. A	16. D	21. C
2. C	7. A	12. C	17. D	22. B
3. C	8. A	13. C	18. C	23. C
4. C	9. B	14. A	19. A	24. A
5. C	10. B	15. B	20. D	25. C

TEST 2

DIRECTIONS: Each question or incomplete statement is followed by several suggested answers or completions. Select the one that BEST answers the question or completes the statement. *PRINT THE LETTER OF THE CORRECT ANSWER IN THE SPACE AT THE RIGHT.*

1. Assume that two very powerful community groups, who have both been very cooperative with park programs, are in disagreement concerning dogs in the park. One group insists that park rules prohibit unleashed dogs, while the other asserts that the rule has never been enforced. Of the following, the BEST course of action for you to take in order to maintain good public relations is to
   A. inform both groups that a special area of the park will be set aside for unleashed dogs
   B. tell both groups that they will have to file written complaints before any action can be taken
   C. tell the group desirous of unleashed dogs that park rules prohibit unleashed animals, but appeals for change may be made
   D. inform the group protesting unleashed dogs that, since the rules has not been strictly enforced in the past, it would be fruitless to try now

1.___

2. Assume that you are meeting with the cabinet of the local office of neighborhood government. These community representatives complain that a certain playground has been repeatedly vandalized. Your men have made repairs at this facility on several occasions.
   Of the following, the MOST effective advice you can give the cabinet about such a situation generally is that
   A. you are short-handed and nothing more can be done
   B. the community has a large responsibility for seeing that park facilities are not vandalized, and suggest that a community group accept responsibility for reporting all vandalism to the police
   C. the cabinet members should write a letter to the mayor
   D. the cabinet should not interfere in the administration of the parks; the parks department is best able to determine how to handle a situation involving vandalism

2.___

3. As a supervisor, you may speak to various groups or organizations about services and activities provided by the district.
   Of the following, the factor normally LEAST necessary for making a successful talk is
   A. a good idea or subject for discussion
   B. useful knowledge of your subject

3.___

C. formal training in the techniques of public speaking
D. a sincere desire and basic ability to express your ideas

4. You have received a letter of complaint from a local resident that a laborer in a playground in the district was rude to her and her children. You have received other complaints about this person in the past.
In the interest of maintaining good community relations, the one of the following actions which it would normally be BEST for you to take is to
   A. investigate, and promptly telephone or write an appropriate response describing what action, if any, you have taken and send a report to the local office
   B. investigate, and send a report to the local office to let the local office decide if any action is appropriate
   C. dismiss the letter as the work of a chronic crank and do nothing; to investigate might annoy your man
   D. file the complaint so that if several similar ones come in, you can take appropriate action in the future

5. Which of the following is MOST likely to project an unfavorable impression of a municipal agency?
If you are
   A. making a telephone call, identify yourself and the organization immediately
   B. dealing with the public, try to make the people feel important
   C. making a visit, do not hesitate to leave your car improperly parked
   D. delivering supplies, obey the speed limit and stay in the right lane when not passing

6. Of the following, two factors upon which good public relations for a municipal agency depend are favorable media coverage and generally
   A. a good service performance record
   B. the scope of services to be provided
   C. the magnitude of the annual budget
   D. the type of equipment used

7. Several groups interested in determining a location for the new baseball diamond have presented their preferences to you. Rather than yield to the loudest group, you have asked the interested groups to make their requests based on facts such as size, accessibility, number of trees that would have to be destroyed, etc.
Of the following, the BEST reason for making your decision based on these factors is that
   A. facts are always easy to obtain
   B. the decision has a basis which can be defended by interested parties
   C. by this method, the loudest group doesn't always win
   D. you can never go wrong by using facts

8. If a person who is using a park facility is treated discourteously by a park employee, the offended person is *generally* likely to think ill of
   A. just that employee
   B. just that employee and his supervisor
   C. the parks department and the city or county
   D. just the park where the incident took place

8.___

9. If a member of the public is seen violating one of the park rules and regulations, the BEST way to stop the person from continuing is generally to
   A. shout loudly at the person, so that he and all others who have seen him will know that his actions violate park rules
   B. approach the person courteously, tell him of his violation, and be willing to answer any question he may have about the rules
   C. inform the person that he is in violation of the rules and must leave the park facilities at once
   D. ignore the violation, since park personnel do not want the reputation of acting like policemen

9.___

10. Park rules and regulations exist to insure that the greatest number of people make the best use of park facilities. Of the following, the responsibility for seeing that the public follows the rules and regulations falls PRIMARILY on
    A. the supervisor alone, since he is usually the highest ranking person
    B. both the supervisor and the park foreman, since they are supervisory personnel
    C. all park employees who have contact with the public
    D. parks department administrators since they are the ones who establish park priorities

10.___

11. The one of the following requirements which is usually necessary for signs to be effective in informing the public of a park regulation is that
    A. the bottom of signs be no more than 4½ feet from the ground
    B. there be as many of the same type of sign as possible
    C. the signs be legibly lettered, with correct spelling and wording
    D. the signs be distributed at random around the park facility

11.___

12. If a lifeguard at a public beach or pool gives one long blast on his whistle, he is
    A. signaling that he is leaving his station in response to an emergency situation
    B. calling the attention of the public to violations of rules and regulations
    C. calling for the attention of the lifeguard chief or lieutenant (not an emergency)
    D. signaling that he is going off duty, and another lifeguard should cover his station

12.___

13. The one of the following conditions which is LEAST 13.___
    necessary to insure that the public uses rubbish baskets
    is that the baskets be
    A. in good physical condition
    B. emptied when full
    C. conspicuously located
    D. distributed randomly throughout the park area

14. If a park facility is kept clean and well-maintained, the 14.___
    rate of vandlism will likely
    A. *be lowered*, since public cooperation is induced by
       well-kept facilities
    B. *be raised*, since vandals prefer to damage a well-
       kept area
    C. *remain the same*, since the upkeep of a facility has
       no effect on the rate of vandalism
    D. *be raised*, since a well-kept facility is easier to
       damage than a poorly-kept facility

15. In addition to planned regular maintenance, the one of 15.___
    the following which is the best way to keep park facili-
    ties at a high level of operating efficiency so the public
    may have the GREATEST use of the facilities is usually to
    A. make frequent and thorough inspections of all facili-
       ties followed by corrective measures when needed
    B. wait for complaints from park facility users since
       manpower is wasted by correcting defects normally
       unnoticed by the public
    C. take corrective action only on complaints made to
       the borough offices, since only these need be con-
       sidered serious
    D. disregard most complaints, since regular maintenance
       corrects all serious defects in park facilities

Directions 16-25.

DIRECTIONS: Questions 16 through 25 are to be answered on the basis
of the information given below and the two tables
which follow. Some of the questions require taking
into consideration the information in one or both of
the two tables and in the following paragraphs. No
question relates to a previous question.

As a General Park Foreman, R. Carson has been newly assigned to
Undulant Memorial Park, District 841. The schedules have been made
up by the previous General Park Foreman for the week of June 30 to
July 6. The park has 500 acres of grass, a wooded picnic area of
200 acres, 4 comfort stations, a surfaced playground area for children, 10 tennis courts, 2 baseball diamonds, 4 softball diamonds,
6 basketball courts, and 100 acres of additional wooded area which
are being converted to picnic grounds. The conversion of the wooded
area is to be completed before July 4th.

The roster of personnel assigned to District 841 includes 1 General Park Foreman, 2 Park Foremen, 9 laborers, 4 attendants (whose activities are restricted to the tennis courts and locker rooms), and 12 seasonal park helpers. The equipment assigned to District 841 includes 1 pickup truck, 1 dump truck, 1 tractor and grass cutting attachment, 2 Toro mowers, and 2 hand mowers.

The operating requirements (weekly scheduled operations which must be met) for District 841 include a daily morning garbage pickup for the picnic area, a twice weekly pickup Monday and Friday for the rest of the District, and a weekly walking pickup of the entire area on Thursday (see Table II). A garbage pickup of the picnic area takes 4 hours and requires the use of 3 men and a dump truck. The garbage pickup for the rest of the district requires the use of that crew for an additional 3 hours. The walking pickup takes 8 hours and requires the use of 6 men and a pickup truck.

The <u>hours of operation</u> for all facilities in District 841 are <u>8 A.M. to 9 P.M.</u> Seasonal park helpers are scheduled to work 6 days per week, and employees in all other titles are scheduled to work 5 days per week. One hour is given for lunch or supper.

TABLE I

TIME SCHEDULE   Periods: From June 23 to June 29

Dept. of Parks   Park: Undulant Memorial Park

District 841

Title	Sat. 6/23	Sun. 6/24	Mon. 6/25	Tues. 6/26	Wed. 6/27	Thurs. 6/28	Fri. 6/29
General Park Foreman	8-5	8-5	8-5	8-5	8-5		
Park Foreman		8-5	8-5	8-5		8-5	8-5
Park Foreman	1-9		1-9		1-9	1-9	1-9
Laborers 3*	8-5		8-5	8-5	8-5	8-5	8-5
Laborers 3		8-5	8-5	8-5	8-5	8-5	
Laborers 3	1-9		1-9		1-9	1-9	1-9
Seasonal Park Helper 3	8-5		8-5	8-5	8-5	8-5	8-5
Seasonal Park Helper 3		8-5	8-5	8-5	8-5	8-5	8-5
Seasonal Park Helper 3	1-9		1-9	1-9	1-9	1-9	1-9
Seasonal Park Helper 3		1-9	1-9	1-9	1-9	1-9	1-9
Attendant 2	10-6	10-6	10-6	10-6	10-6		
Attendant 2	10-6	10-6			10-6	10-6	10-6

LEGEND
 *Number of employees in that title on that time schedule
   8-5 Tour of duty from 8 A.M. to 5 P.M. (8-hour shift)
   1-9 Tour of duty from 1 P.M. to 9 P.M. (7-hour shift)
   10-6 Tour of duty from 10 A.M. to 6 P.M. (7-hour shift)

TABLE II

OPERATING REQUIREMENTS

EQUIPMENT	Sat. 6/23	Sun. 6/24	Mon. 6/25	Tues. 6/26	Wed. 6/27	Thurs. 6/28	Fri. 6/29
Pickup Truck						6 / 8	
Dump Truck	3 / 4	3 / 4	3 / 7	3 / 4	3 / 4	3 / 4	3 / 7

LEGEND

number of men / hours men and equipment employed

16. A man using the tractor with grass-cutting equipment can cut an average of ten acres of grass per hour; with a Toro mower, 4 acres per hour; and with a hand mower, 1 acre per hour. Only 250 of the 400 acres of grass can be cut with the tractor.
The total number of **man-hours** (one man-hour is defined as one hour of work for one man) it will take to cut all 500 acres of grass using all the available machinery simultaneously is MOST NEARLY
    A. 50 B. 100 C. 125 D. 200

17. The conversion of the wooded area to picnic grounds is complete except for the installation of 100 additional picnic tables. It is estimated that this project requires the use of a pickup truck and 2 men for 40 hours. Because this is a priority item, it will be worked on during all the hours the park is open.
If the project must be completed by Friday noon for the 4th of July holiday, considering that the operating requirements listed in Table II must be met, we would expect the project to begin
    A. Saturday afternoon   B. Sunday morning
    C. Monday afternoon   D. Tuesday afternoon

18. Assuming that all the operating requirements must be met, of the following, the day on which there will NOT be a sufficient number of men available to install baseball and softball backstops, a project requiring the simultaneous use of 8 men for 7 hours is
    A. Saturday   B. Monday   C. Thursday   D. Friday

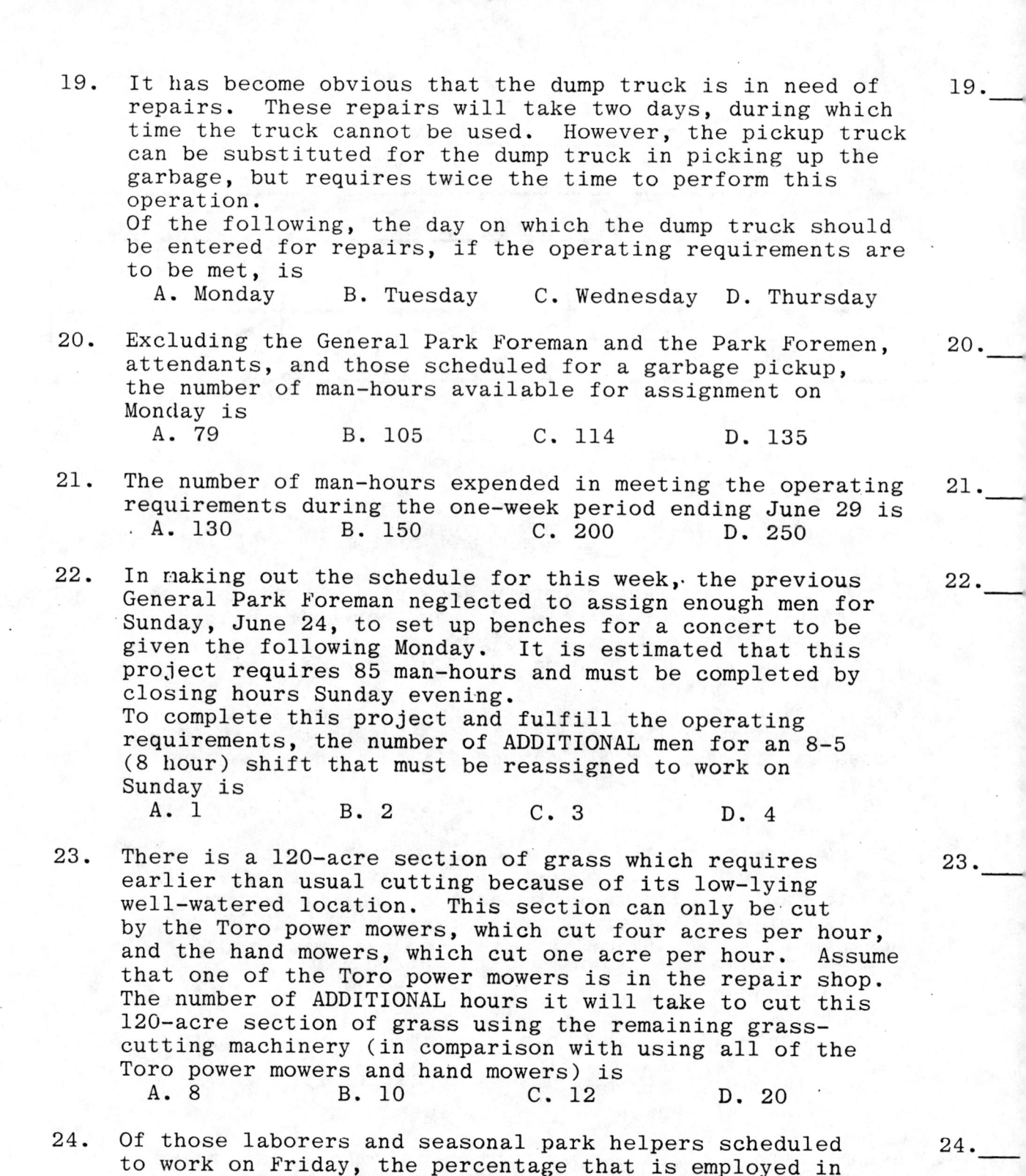

19. It has become obvious that the dump truck is in need of repairs. These repairs will take two days, during which time the truck cannot be used. However, the pickup truck can be substituted for the dump truck in picking up the garbage, but requires twice the time to perform this operation.
    Of the following, the day on which the dump truck should be entered for repairs, if the operating requirements are to be met, is
    A. Monday   B. Tuesday   C. Wednesday   D. Thursday

20. Excluding the General Park Foreman and the Park Foremen, attendants, and those scheduled for a garbage pickup, the number of man-hours available for assignment on Monday is
    A. 79   B. 105   C. 114   D. 135

21. The number of man-hours expended in meeting the operating requirements during the one-week period ending June 29 is
    A. 130   B. 150   C. 200   D. 250

22. In making out the schedule for this week, the previous General Park Foreman neglected to assign enough men for Sunday, June 24, to set up benches for a concert to be given the following Monday. It is estimated that this project requires 85 man-hours and must be completed by closing hours Sunday evening.
    To complete this project and fulfill the operating requirements, the number of ADDITIONAL men for an 8-5 (8 hour) shift that must be reassigned to work on Sunday is
    A. 1   B. 2   C. 3   D. 4

23. There is a 120-acre section of grass which requires earlier than usual cutting because of its low-lying well-watered location. This section can only be cut by the Toro power mowers, which cut four acres per hour, and the hand mowers, which cut one acre per hour. Assume that one of the Toro power mowers is in the repair shop. The number of ADDITIONAL hours it will take to cut this 120-acre section of grass using the remaining grass-cutting machinery (in comparison with using all of the Toro power mowers and hand mowers) is
    A. 8   B. 10   C. 12   D. 20

24. Of those laborers and seasonal park helpers scheduled to work on Friday, the percentage that is employed in fulfilling the operating requirements is MOST NEARLY
    A. 8.2   B. 16.6   C. 23.8   D. 37.5

25. For scheduling purposes, the General Park Foreman must know how long it will take to complete the garbage collection on Monday, June 25, if both the dump truck and the pickup truck are used.
If the pickup truck takes twice as long as the dump truck in collecting garbage, the number of hours it takes to collect the garbage using both trucks is MOST NEARLY
   A. 2.1   B. 3.2   C. 4.7   D. 6.3

KEY (CORRECT ANSWERS)

1. C	11. C
2. B	12. A
3. C	13. D
4. A	14. A
5. C	15. A
6. A	16. C
7. B	17. C
8. C	18. A
9. B	19. B
10. C	20. C

21. B
22. D
23. A
24. B
25. C

EXAMINATION SECTION
TEST 1

DIRECTIONS: Each question or incomplete statement is followed by several suggested answers or completions. Select the one that BEST answers the question or completes the statement. *PRINT THE LETTER OF THE CORRECT ANSWER IN THE SPACE AT THE RIGHT.*

1. Assume that a park employee from another district asks you about possible transfers exchanging him and an employee in your district. The two have already discussed it and would like to change.
   For you to DENY such a request is

   A. *advisable;* employees should learn to adjust to their assignments and no one should expect preferential treatment
   B. *inadvisable;* denial may lower work quality and morale when unusual circumstances may be the reason for desiring a change
   C. *inadvisable;* employee requests for transfers always improve work performance of an entire crew
   D. *advisable;* such transfers are never effective and always seem to begin an endless cycle of transfers

   1.____

2. An employee, whom you have reprimanded for low level performance, as begun to work at a level above average.
   For you to PRAISE the employee at least once weekly is a

   A. *good* practice, mainly because the employee will always produce at a higher rate if he know his work is appreciated
   B. *poor* practice, mainly because praise should only be given for an unusually high level of performance
   C. *good* practice, mainly because lack of praise probably caused his low level of performance
   D. *poor* practice, mainly because too much praise seems to lack sincerity

   2.____

3. A laborer reports to you that the park foreman, to whom he is responsible, drinks beer and wine on the job. He states that the foreman's orders are unclear, that he treats his subordinates in an inhumane manner, and he sleeps on the job frequently
   Of the following, the MOST proper action for you to take in this situation is to

   A. tell the employee that you see the foreman every day and he is never intoxicated
   B. ask the employee to keep a secret record of such occurrences and report to you at the end of the month
   C. approach this foreman, along with the laborer who made the complaint, inform him of the allegation, and allow the two to debate the issues
   D. observe this foreman more frequently to discover if the allegation is true and what remedial action need be taken

   3.____

4. You have given a special assignment to an emergency roving work crew to report to a bridge across the horse trail to do some repair work. Of the following, such an order is generally

   4.____

A. *good;* the work order permits the general park supervisor to determine exactly the effectiveness of the roving crew
B. *poor;* the work order tells the crew nothing about the nature, equipment, or manpower needed for the repair
C. *good;* roving crews only need to be told where to go and no further details are necessary
D. *poor;* the general park supervisor should not have to tell the roving crew about a repair, since they should know about it first

5. It is one of your responsibilities to schedule the work hours of all the parks employees in your district.
Of the following, for you to discuss a schedule with your subordinate foremen informally before making it final is generally

   A. *undesirable,* since scheduling is your responsibility and you must not let others influence you in carrying it out
   B. *desirable,* since your subordinates are more likely to accept the schedule if they have had some part in its construction
   C. *undesirable,* since too many conflicting ideas will be received which you cannot resolve
   D. *desirable,* since the blame for any errors in the schedule can be spread among several people

6. A supervisor often gives directives in the form of suggestions rather than as formal orders.
This practice is generally

   A. *desirable,* since a series of formal orders may produce resistance from subordinates
   B. *undesirable,* since suggestions would show indecisiveness
   C. *desirable,* since a supervisor should always act in a friendly manner
   D. *undesirable,* since suggestions would not have to be taken seriously

7. Of the following, the BEST statement about the *grapevine* as a form of communication is that it is

   A. *always destructive* of organization since it only carries gossip and false information
   B. *always useful* because it usually provides more accurate information than formal channels of communication
   C. *often useful* because it provides a channel of communication for information which formal lines of communication cannot suitably carry
   D. *never destructive* of organization since it is only used for harmless, idle gossip

8. The manner in which a supervisor directs his workers usually influences the amount of work which the workers do.
Of the following, workers are MOST likely to produce more work under a supervisor who assigns a job,

   A. instructs in detail how the job is to be done, and closely watches that the job is performed in that way
   B. and leaves it to the workers to figure out how the job is to be done, and checks up only when the job is finished

C. instructs in detail how the job is to be done, and checks the work only when the job is finished
D. leaves the workers to perform it as he has trained them to, and checks occasionally to see that the job is being performed adequately

9. An essential piece of equipment has developed a serious mechanical problem. It can be operated in a limited manner, but will eventually have to go to the district shop for a few weeks for major repairs. Before deciding whether you will have the machine repaired at once or use it as it is for a while, you wish to confer with your foremen. Two of your foremen, however, are new and inexperienced.
Of the following, the BEST statement about including them in the meeting is that such action is generally

   A. *desirable,* since such a meeting will give the men a change from their ordinary work
   B. *undesirable,* since these inexperienced men can contribute nothing and would be just wasting time
   C. *desirable,* since such a meeting with experienced men provides these inexperienced men with an opportunity to learn
   D. *undesirable,* since any ideas offered by these inexperienced men can only confuse the meeting

10. The maintenance of good employee morale is important to high production.
The existence of legitimate grievance channels through which an employee may effectively express dissatisfaction nornally tends, in the long run, to _____ the number of grievances.

   A. *raise* morale while *diminishing*
   B. *lower* morale while *increasing*
   C. *have no effect* on morale or
   D. *raise* morale while *increasing*

11. While making your rounds in the district, you find that one of your men is making a mistake which is clearly due to negligence on his part.
Of the following, your BEST course of action normally is to

   A. reprimand the man at once, loudly, so that other employees in the area will know that you will not tolerate such mistakes
   B. talk to the man privately, letting him know in strong terms that you are personally very angry with him for such performance since it reflects on your superiors' view of you
   C. reprimand the man, then, for several days after, remind him that you are checking his performance so that he will not repeat his negligence
   D. use the situation to train the employee in proper procedure and point out to him the bad effects of negligent work

12. A laborer with an otherwise good work history often comes in late. You ask him why, and he answers, *I just can't get up in the morning. Frankly, I've just lost interest in the job; when I do get up, I've got to rush like crazy to get here.*
Which of the following responses from you would MOST likely lead to a constructive solution of the problem?

A. You don't know what an alarm clock is?
B. Are you having problems with your family?
C. Why have you lost interest in the job?
D. Well, that's no reason for coming in late.

13. A worker over 50 will generally be better than a worker under 25 in all of the following areas EXCEPT

    A. frequency of absences
    B. length of sick-leave absences
    C. safety record
    D. number of grievances

14. Of the following, the advantage for a supervisor in delegating his authority is that such delegation normally provides him with a means to

    A. devote his own time to the more important aspects of a job and assign the less important aspects to his subordinates
    B. keep close personal control over all details in his district
    C. restrict a subordinate's freedom to make wrong decisions
    D. earn his subordinates' respect by working alongside them at the same job

15. In preparing general assignments and work schedules of a group of employees, a supervisor can generally expect the BEST results by making assignments according to which one of the following?

    A. A method which always places workers with similar skills together
    B. A method which takes into account the personalities of the group members
    C. Group preference, which will usually lead to high quality output
    D. A method which does not involve personality factors

16. Workers separated by great distances from the source of authority at the top of the organization have difficulty in *communicating upward.*
    Upward communication MOST NEARLY means

    A. directives that originate with top officials
    B. messages relayed from lower levels to management
    C. communication among workers
    D. a worker's ability to understand formally written orders

17. An angry public works employee tells you about a vending machine concessionaire who has thrown his litter onto the area recently cleaned by the employee. Upon investigation, you discover that the wastebaskets provided for the concessionaire, for which the worker is responsible, are filled to capacity.
    Of the following, the BEST course for you to take in this situation is to

    A. tell the employee that his failure to perform his work is the cause of the trouble; he must improve immediately or be fired
    B. call attention to the employee's poor work record and tell him that he has caused you personal embarrassment
    C. console the employee, tell him that the vendor or another employee is at fault
    D. tell the employee that he should be sure the baskets are properly emptied and if he performs his work correctly, such problems will be eliminated

18. The efficiency of an employee depends in part on the type and quality of training he receives.
    Of the following, the BEST method for you to use to train new laborers during a period when personnel is short is to train them

    A. only for the immediate job operation
    B. for more than one operation only if they had prior experience
    C. on a continuous basis so that immediate and long-range job operations are considered
    D. by giving all the details of the job operation during the first training session

    18.____

19. A park foreman has indicated to you that a major steel connector on a basketball court in the district needs to be replaced. You then later discover that the extent of the damage on the court requires the removal of the damaged connector immediately.
    Of the following, the BEST way to have the connector replaced is for you to report the situation first to the

    A. roving work crew who is directly responsible for all emergencies
    B. regular work crew who is directly responsible for the area
    C. mechanical shop who will replace the connector
    D. senior supervisor of park operations who is directly responsible for property damage

    19.____

20. Assume that you were told of a minor incident involving one of the workers and a teenage boy in the park. The following day, you overhear the true details of the incident which were much more serious than those which you were told.
    Why is it that information originating at the lowest level of an organization often reaches higher levels in a completely different form?

    A. Workers at the lowest levels in an organization usually enjoy deceiving their superiors.
    B. Workers often feel that supervisors are their enemy and, therefore, they prefer to keep any information about themselves within their own ranks.
    C. Information starting at the lower levels tends to be stripped of details which might anger or upset the immediate supervisor.
    D. Most supervisors are too busy to be hindered by disciplinary reports about their workers.

    20.____

21. While he is preparing for a rock concert expected to draw a capacity crowd, an employee scheduled to assist with the affair is injured. From past experience, you know that Bill is the best replacement for the injured employee.
    Of the following, the MOST appropriate action for you to take is to

    A. approach Bill as you would any friend, pointing out your faith in him
    B. tell Bill that you know that someone else is available, but that he is so fussy that you'd rather have him, since he always knows what to do
    C. give Bill an order stating that he will replace the injured employee
    D. tell Bill what has happened so that he understands why he is being asked to work and make him feel that he has a part in an important decision

    21.____

22. Following a two-month period of regular inspection procedures and a number of discussions with the foreman and individual laborers about proper maintenance procedures, you still receive complaints from patrons about substandard maintenance of the area adjacent to a swimming pool in your district.
The one of the following which is the MOST appropriate action for you to take is to

    A. hold private sessions with each laborer to find out how to correct the situation
    B. hold a group conference to express your dissatisfaction in clear terms and to give the work crew a chance to present their side of the issue
    C. complain to your superiors to get help concerning the best method of improvement
    D. hold a group conference, calling only upon members of the crew who have performed satisfactorily for improvement ideas

23. Assume that you want to train a new park foreman by rotating him to all blotter stops in your district so he will receive on-the-job training from experienced park foremen. You also plan to hold daily sessions with the new foreman.
Of the following, the MOST correct statement about this procedure is that it is generally

    A. *undesirable;* the new foreman would not know what to do with so many people directing him
    B. *desirable;* a person in the same job position as the new employee would always be helpful
    C. *desirable;* the new foreman would receive varied and needed experience along with supervisory attention
    D. *undesirable;* a person in the same job position always resents new persons and does not properly train them

24. An employee complains to you about what he feels is the overbearing conduct of the park foreman who is his superior.
Of the following, the MOST immediate action that you should generally take is to

    A. reprimand the foreman immediately and demand that he adhere to a more democratic method of supervision
    B. investigate the situation since an employee usually does not find it easy to complain about his superior
    C. dismiss the allegation since most employees enjoy creating problems for others, especially for their superiors
    D. defend the foreman, reminding the employee that the foreman has the proper knowledge and experience to handle his position efficiently

25. During the past three weeks, Frank Parker, usually an efficient employee, has developed an unusual attitude and frequently *pops off* in the presence of other workers. His work performance has fallen below the accepted standard and his attitude has lowered the morale of his work team.
Of the following, the BEST action for you to take is to

    A. reprimand Frank by reminding him that neither his attitude nor his poor work will be tolerated
    B. call Frank in for a conference to discuss his work performance
    C. ignore Frank's behavior, since he has performed well in the past
    D. transfer Frank to other work locations at set intervals, to keep his morale and work standards up

KEY (CORRECT ANSWERS)

1. B
2. D
3. D
4. B
5. B

6. A
7. C
8. D
9. C
10. A

11. D
12. C
13. B
14. A
15. B

16. B
17. D
18. C
19. C
20. C

21. D
22. B
23. C
24. B
25. B

TEST 2

DIRECTIONS: Each question or incomplete statement is followed by several suggested answers or completions. Select the one that BEST answers the question or completes the statement. *PRINT THE LETTER OF THE CORRECT ANSWER IN THE SPACE AT THE RIGHT.*

1. Which of the following is the MOST likely action a supervisor should take to help establish an effective working relationship with his departmental superiors?

    A. Delay the implementation of new procedures received from superiors in order to evaluate their appropriateness
    B. Skip the chain of command whenever he feels that it is to his advantage
    C. Keep supervisors informed of problems in his area and the steps taken to correct them
    D. Don't take up superiors' time by discussing anticipated problems but wait until the difficulties occur

2. Of the following, the action a supervisor could take which would generally be MOST conducive to the establishment of an effective working relationship with employees includes

    A. maintaining impersonal relationships to prevent development of biased actions
    B. treating all employees equally without adjusting for individual differences
    C. continuous observation of employees on the job with insistence on constant improvement
    D. careful planning and scheduling of work for your employees

3. Which of the following procedures is the LEAST likely to establish effective working relationships between employees and supervisors?

    A. Encouraging *two-way* communication with employees
    B. Periodic discussion with employees regarding their job performance
    C. Ignoring employees' gripes concerning job difficulties
    D. Avoiding personal prejudices in dealing with employees

4. Criticism can be used as a tool to point out the weak areas of a subordinate's work performance.
    Of the following, the BEST action for a supervisor to take so that his criticism will be accepted is to

    A. focus his criticism on the act instead of on the person
    B. exaggerate the errors in order to motivate the employee to do better
    C. pass judgment quickly and privately, without investigating the circumstances of the error
    D. generalize the criticism and not specifically point out the errors in performance

5. Assume that it has come to your attention that two of your subordinates have shouted at each other and have almost engaged in a fist fight; luckily, they were separated by some of the other employees.
    Of the following, your BEST immediate course of action would generally be to

A. reprimand the senior of the two subordinates, since he should have known better
B. hear the story from both employees and any witnesses and then take needed disciplinary action
C. ignore the matter, since nobody was physically hurt
D. immediately suspend and fine both employees pending a departmental hearing

6. You have been delegating some of your authority to one of your subordinates because of his leadership potential.
Which of the following actions is LEAST conducive to the growth and development of this individual for a supervisory position?

    A. Use praise only when it will be effective
    B. Give very detailed instructions and supervise the employee closely to be sure that the instructions are followed precisely
    C. Let the subordinate proceed with his planned course of action even if mistakes, within a permissible range, are made
    D. Intervene on behalf of the subordinate whenever an assignment becomes difficult for him

7. A rumor has been spreading in your department concerning the possibility of layoffs due to decreased revenues.
As a supervisor, you should generally

    A. deny the rumor, whether it is true or false, in order to keep morale from declining
    B. inform the men to the best of your knowledge about this situation and keep them advised of any new information
    C. tell the men to forget about the rumor and concentrate on increasing their productivity
    D. ignore the rumor, since it is not authorized information

8. Within an organization, every supervisor should know to whom he reports and who reports to him.
The one of the following which is achieved by use of such structured relationships is

    A. unity of command   B. confidentiality
    C. esprit de corps   D. promotion opportunities

9. While observing a summer aide perform his duties, you notice that he is using many useless motions in completing a task.
In order to improve the productivity of the aid, you generally can BEST use this opportunity to

    A. reprimand the aide for his inefficient performance
    B. point out the aide's inefficiency and compare this performance to other mistakes he has committed, in order to motivate him
    C. provide training for the aide at this time in order to increase his future work productivity
    D. let the aide learn by doing

10. While spot-checking the activities of summer park aides, you notice a few of them engaging in *horseplay*.
Of the following, the MOST appropriate action for you to take would be to

A. tell the summer park aides to immediately stop the *horseplay* and continue with their work
B. ignore their actions if their work is progressing satisfactorily; after all, *horseplay* is normal among youthful employees
C. reprimand the aides by telling them to go home for the day
D. report this incident to the aides' immediate supervisor when you see him

11. Of the following, the action of a supervisor that would be LEAST likely to give the general public a favorable impression of the parks department would be to

    A. provide information concerning the department's interest in community affairs
    B. acquaint friends and others with departmental activities that provide a favorable view of the department
    C. speak unfavorably of the working conditions established by the department
    D. participate in and support civic and community activities

12. Assume that it has come to your attention that small amounts of minor park supplies and materials have been disappearing.
    Of the following, the BEST statement about ignoring this situation is that to do so is

    A. *desirable;* since no large thefts have occurred, it would be better to forget about the little items
    B. *desirable;* since the work is being done, there is no reason to upset the workers
    C. *undesirable;* the park may have to close due to the thefts of supplies
    D. *undesirable;* you would be condoning such acts unless you take immediate steps to curtail these occurrences

13. Several members of a work crew have approached you with the idea of rotating men on job assignments such as raking leaves, picking up paper, and making minor repairs on the tennis courts.
    Of the following, your BEST answer would be:

    A. I'm sorry, but such a change would make it impossible to keep track of who does what
    B. If you all agree to the change, let's try it
    C. I'm not sure if that is allowed. I'll send in some papers and notify you in a couple of weeks
    D. The work is getting done now. Leave things as they are

14. Which of the following is generally the MOST effective way for you to communicate information to the workers?

    A. Face-to-face communication
    B. A notice on the bulletin board
    C. The telephone
    D. A messenger with a memo

15. While walking through the playground, you find one of the workers sitting on a park bench. He has done an excellent job of cleaning the area; and when you approach him, he says that he is *just taking a short break.*
    Of the following, the MOST acceptable course of action for you to take in this situation is to

A. tell him there is plenty of work still to be done
B. tell him to save his rests for lunch breaks
C. pretend that you don't see him
D. tell him that he is entitled to a quick break because he has done a good job, but to make it a small break

16. Assume that you have found out that one of the workers usually drinks alcohol heavily on his lunch hour.
Of the following, the BEST course of action for you to take in such a situation is to

A. try to isolate him so that he will not influence the other workers
B. call his wife and ask her for her help
C. tactfully suggest that he seek professional help
D. try to find the cause of his problem and help him solve it

17. Penetrating oil is OFTEN used for

A. cutting pipe
B. loosening rusted bolts
C. clearing clogged pipes
D. lubricating electric appliances

18. Sweating or condensation of moisture on the outside of a pipe is MOST likely to occur on _____ pipes.

A. hot water
B. steam
C. cold water
D. compressed air

19. Turpentine may be used as a thinner for

A. shellac
B. latex paints
C. calcimine
D. oil paints

20. Creosote is COMMONLY used to

A. preserve wood from rot
B. fireproof wood structures
C. change the color of wood
D. hasten the seasoning of wood

21. The MOST commonly used welding torches are fed by two tanks of gas.
One of these tanks holds acetylene and the other holds

A. carbon dioxide
B. hydrogen
C. nitrogen
D. oxygen

22. When 8-32 is used to designate a screw, the figures represent, respectively,

A. threads/inch and diameter
B. length and diameter
C. diameter and length
D. diameter and threads/inch

23. Galvanized pipe has a finish coating of

A. lead   B. zinc   C. copper   D. nickel

24. It is not considered good practice to paint portable wooden ladders. Of the following, the MOST logical reason for this is that the

    A. painted rungs would become slippery when wet
    B. paint might rub off on a supporting wall
    C. paint might hide serious defects
    D. paint would quickly wear off

25. The type of fastener MOST commonly used when bolting to concrete uses a(n)

    A. expansion shield   B. U-bolt
    C. toggle bolt   D. turnbuckle

KEY (CORRECT ANSWERS)

1.	C	11.	C
2.	D	12.	D
3.	C	13.	B
4.	A	14.	A
5.	B	15.	D
6.	B	16.	C
7.	B	17.	B
8.	A	18.	C
9.	C	19.	D
10.	A	20.	A

21. D
22. D
23. B
24. C
25. A

EXAMINATION SECTION

DIRECTIONS: Each question or incomplete statement is followed by several suggested answers or completions. Select the one that BEST answers the question or completes the statement. *PRINT THE LETTER OF THE CORRECT ANSWER IN THE SPACE AT THE RIGHT.*

1. A type of depression or pit that may serve to drain, collect or store liquids is called a
    A. ditch   B. gutter   C. sump   D. trench

    1._____

2. The general name applied to the material that is spread on the ground around plants to prevent evaporation of water from the soil or the freezing of the roots is
    A. mulch   B. mullock   C. fertilizer   D. mullion

    2._____

3. The wire, rope, chain or rod that is attached to a tree, and which is used to steady the tree, is called a
    A. guy   B. davit   C. hoist   D. bitt

    3._____

4. A chemical used to kill weeds is called a
    A. pesticide   B. herbicide   C. fungicide   D. arborcide

    4._____

5. A mixture of cement or lime with sand and water which is used between bricks or stones in buildings is called
    A. epoxy   B. putty   C. concrete   D. mortar

    5._____

6. Coarse aggregate is the same as
    A. pumice   B. cement
    C. crushed stone   D. sand

    6._____

7. The process of keeping the surface of concrete as wet as possible after the concrete is placed and hardened in order to prevent loss of water through evaporation is called
    A. floating   B. damping   C. curing   D. checking

    7._____

8. Plants that live for more than two years are called
    A. annuals   B. perennials   C. biennials   D. semi-annuals

    8._____

9. Which piece of equipment is run by compressed air?
    A. Drill press   B. Impact wrench
    C. Soldering gun   D. Jack hammer

    9._____

QUESTIONS 10-13.
Answer questions 10-13 SOLELY on the basis of the information given in the paragraphs below.

NITROGEN AND PLANT GROWTH

Nitrogen is an essential element for plant growth. Its most important function is to stimulate vegatative development and it is, therefore particularly necessary in the production of leaves and stems. If an excess of nitrogen is applied to the soil, it will result in an excessive growth of foliage at the expense of flowers and fruit. The cell walls of the stems will also become weakened and the plant's resistance to disease will be lowered.

Nitrogen is seldom found in the soil in a free state but is usually combination with other elements. Soils are usually lowest in available nitrogen during the early spring months. It is at this season that quickly available nitrogenous fertilizers are of particular value.

10. According to the paragraph, an excess of nitrogen in plants is *likely to* produce
    A. strong healthy stems
    B. stronger resistance to disease
    C. too many leaves and stems
    D. too many flowers and fruit

11. Weakened cell walls and decreased resistance to disease in plants are *likely to* occur because
    A. there is too much foliage on the plant
    B. there is not enough nitrogen in the soil
    C. there is too much nitrogen in the soil
    D. there are too many flowers or too much fruit on the plant

12. According to the above passage, one of the properties of nitrogen is that it
    A. seldom combines with other elements in the soil
    B. increase the production of flowers
    C. increases the growth of roots
    D. increases vegetative growth in a plant

13. In which months would soil *most likely* be LOWEST in nitrogen? Late
    A. March and early April
    B. June and early July
    C. September and early October
    D. December and early January

14. A person may appear to be accident-prone for a number of reasons.
    Which of the following would NOT usually be particularly associated with frequent accidents?
    A. Slow work habits
    B. Improper training
    C. Lack of physical coordination
    D. Working in cramped quarters

15. When removing a large branch from a tree, a pruner usually 15.____
includes an undercut on the branch.
The SPECIFIC purpose of the undercut is to
   A. stimulate the flow of sap to the area where the branch is taken off in order to stimulate growth of new branches
   B. prevent the branch that is being taken off from tearing off a strip of bark down the tree
   C. aid the wound from the cut off branch to heal quickly without decay or infection
   D. prevent an excessive growth of new branches from where the branch had been

16. A foreman sees one of his men start to cut a hedge so that 16.____
it will be narrower at the bottom than at the top. The foreman stops the man and tells him to cut hedges in general so that they are narrower at the top than at the bottom. "Why?" asks the man.
The foreman gave him the *generally accepted* reason, which is that
   A. rainfall will be able to run down the sides, and moisture will reach other parts of the hedge more quickly
   B. the broad base of the hedge will keep the hedge from being top-heavy and prevent it from toppling over during heavy winds
   C. sunlight will be able to reach all parts of the hedge, thereby helping to keep the growth of the entire hedge dense
   D. the hedge will be uniform from top to bottom since the top grows out much faster than the bottom

17. Concrete sidewalks are usually laid with a divider space 17.____
every four or six feet rather than as one long ribbon.
The reason for allowing the space is that in the summer the concrete in the sidewalk is *most likely* to
   A. contract   B. expand   C. sweat   D. soften

18. Some degree of shock accompanies all injuries. Symptoms 18.____
of shock include all of the following EXCEPT
   A. a warm dry skin   B. a rapid, weak pulse
   C. enlarged pupils   D. irregular breathing

19. You are going to plant ivy in the circular flower bed pic- 19.____
tured in Figure I. You have decided to plant them on the border of each of circles A, B, and C. The distance around each of the circles is as follows:

   A = 32 feet

   B = 20 feet

   C = 6 feet

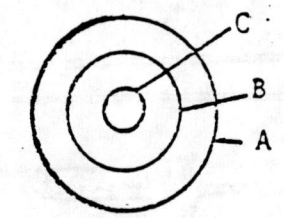

FIGURE I

If you can plant 3 plants per foot, how many plants will you need?
   A. 100   B. 135   C. 156   D. 174

20. Nine out of ten people have never used a fire extinguisher. 20.____
A trained person used a fire extinguisher 2½ times more effectively than the average person does.
These facts should motivate a foreman of a new crew exposed to possible fire hazards to
    A. have a substitute for fire extinguishers on the job
    B. rely only on experienced firemen for extinguishing fires
    C. try to get men into his crew who are experienced in the use of fire extinguighers
    D. give training to his men on the use of fire extinguishers

21. The crowbar, pick and shovel are three hand tools that can 21.____
all be used *effectively* and *safely* in the process of
    A. splitting logs   B. prying heavy objects
    C. making holes in stone   D. digging up earth

22. Those tools which require the user to twist or turn one 22.____
end in one direction while the other end is held fast in order to apply a force on an object are classified as torsion tools.
Of the following, the one which would NOT be classified as a torsion tool is
    A. pliers   B. wrench   C. pinchbar   D. screw driver

23. A portable heater used widely in severe weather to protect 23.____
masonry, concrete and plaster from freezing and to provide warmth for workmen is the
    A. blowtorch   B. salamander
    C. plumbers' furnace   D. metal forge

24. In loading and unloading materials a variety of equipment 24.____
is used.
Of the following, the one which is generally NOT an accessory in moving materials onto and off trucks is a
    A. power shovel   B. clam shell
    C. grease rack   D. lift truck

25. Which one of the following pictures shows the top of a 25.____
Phillips-type screw?

26. Which one of the following is called a box-end wrench? 26.____

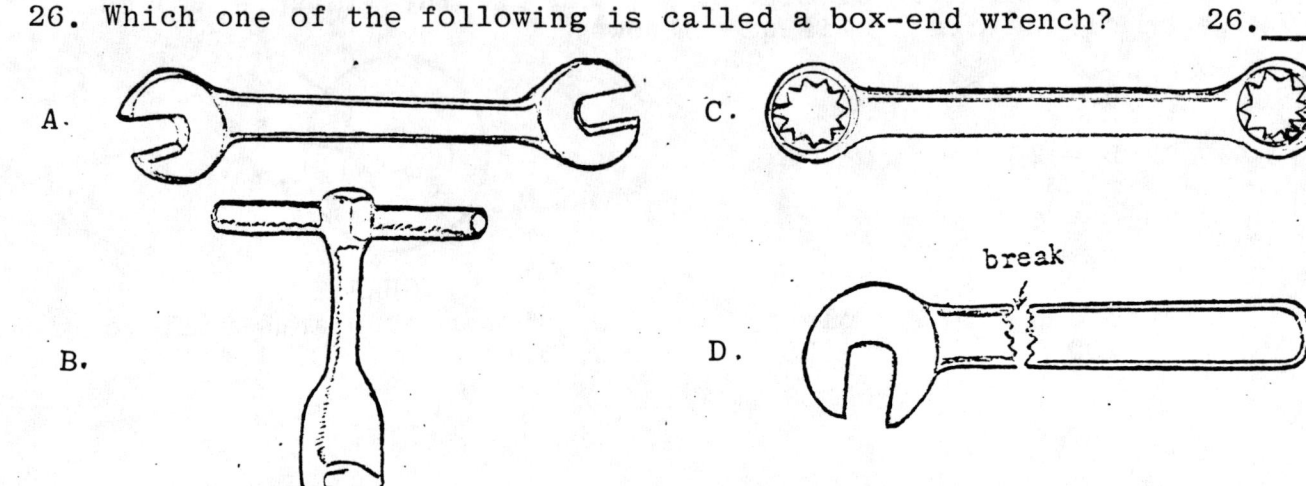

27. A chisel is a hammer-struck tool. Some workmen grip the   27._____
    chisel with the fist to steady it and minimize the chances
    of glancing blows. The turn "glancing" refers here to the
    A. hammer striking the chisel off angle, thereby hitting the
       hand holding the chisel
    B. chisel bending or warping under the pressure of hammer
       blows
    C. hammer hitting with uneven force each time it contacts
       the chisel
    D. chisel striking the material to be cut straight on,
       instead of at an angle

28. Which one of the following BEST describes a *countersink*? A 28._____
    A. tool designed to balance weight
    B. hammer used to shape sheet metal
    C. tool that enlarges the top part of a hole
    D. tool used to dig holes rapidly

29. Of the following, the MAIN reason that some electrical   29._____
    tools require the use of a 3-pronged plug is to
    A. prolong the life of the fuse
    B. avoid wasting electricity
    C. prolong the life of the cord
    D. properly ground them

30. Which of the following statements applies BEST to the care 30._____
    and use of a shovel?
    A. A shovel should not be waxed or greased immediately
       before using it.
    B. Dipping a shovel into a pail of water occasionally,
       while digging, makes the shovel easier to use.
    C. The leg muscles should not be permitted to take most of
       the load when shovelling.
    D. A shovel should lie flat on the ground when it is not
       being used.

31. Which is the SAFEST distance between the base of a 24-foot 31._____
    fully extended ladder and the base of the building against
    which it is placed?
    A. 3 feet   B. 6 feet   C. 9 feet   D. 12 feet

32. When instructing a man on how to lift a heavy object, you 32._____
    should advise him to
    A. stand as far from the load as possible
    B. keep the back as straight as possible
    C. lift by straightening his legs first and then his back
    D. lift from a full crouch

33. Suppose that, of 14 men assigned to a shop, 3 are absent. 33._____
    The percentage of men absent is, *most nearly*,
    A. 19%   B. 20%   C. 21%   D. 22%

34. The sum of 5 1/6 + 7 1/3 + 4¼ + 3 1/8 is   34._____
    A. 19 7/8   B. 20¼   C. 20 3/4   D. 20 7/8

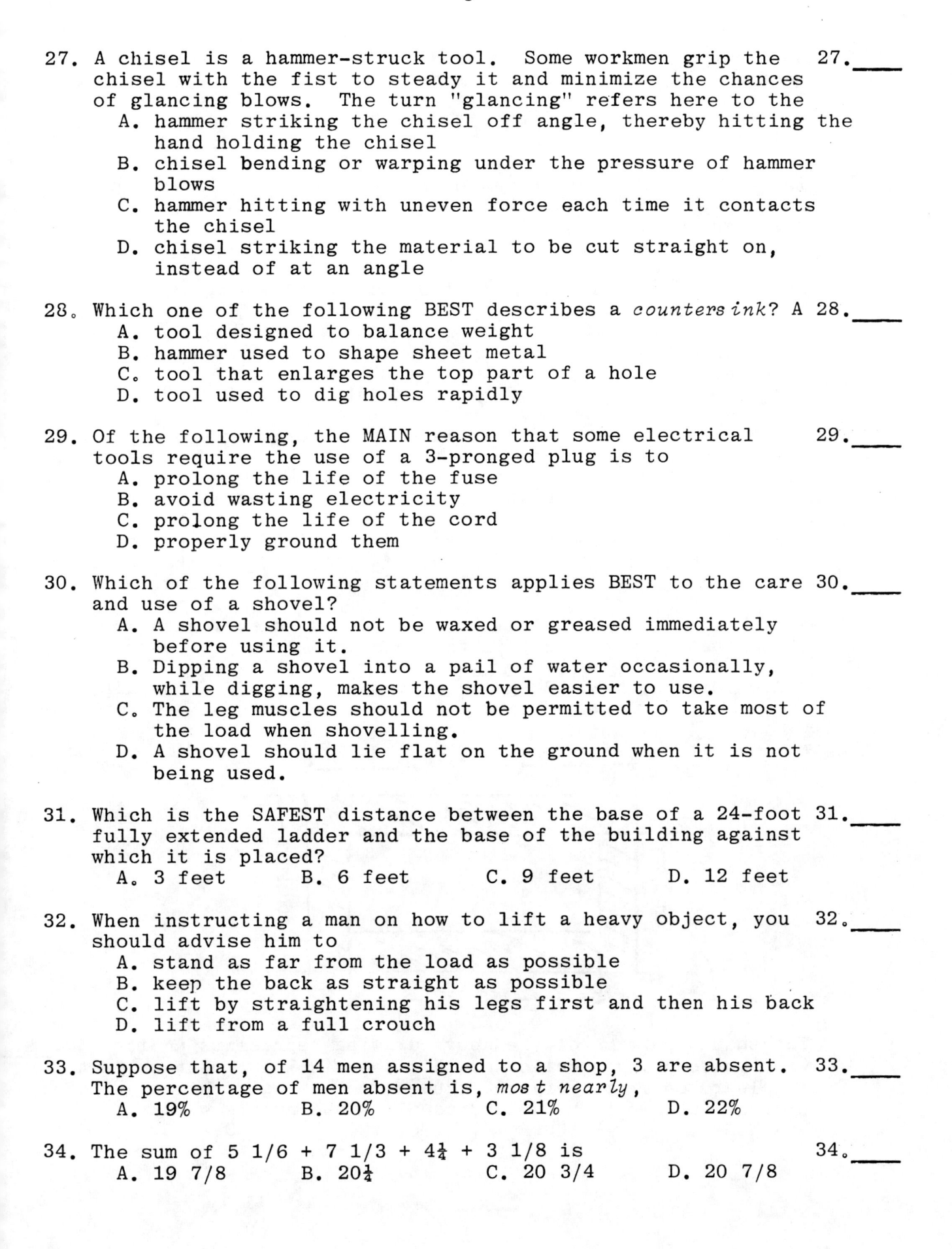

35. A foreman must order enough sod to cover a dirt area 36 feet wide by 28 feet long. Each piece of sod is 3 feet long by 12 inches wide.
How many pieces of sod should be ordered to cover that area?
   A. 192   B. 236   C. 304   D. 336

36. If each man works at the same speed and 6 men take 2½ hours to do a particular job, how many men will it take to do the same job in 1 hour?
   A. 13   B. 15   C. 26   D. 30

37. An agency bought 115 hammers from Company A for $253.00. It later bought 80 hammers from Company B for $140.00 If the agency had bought all of its hammers from Company B, the TOTAL AMOUNT of money that would have been saved would have been
   A. $25.25   B. $45.00   C. $51.75   D. $63.25

38. In order to make up a particular mixture of concrete, a foreman mixes 2 parts of cement to 3 parts of sand and 4 parts of gravel.
If he wants to make up 405 lbs. of concrete, he would need
   A. 45 lbs. of cement, 170 lbs. of sand, and 190 lbs. of gravel
   B. 45 lbs. of cement, 160 lbs. of sand, and 200 lbs. of gravel
   C. 90 lbs. of cement, 140 lbs. of sand, and 175 lbs. of gravel
   D. 90 lbs. of cement, 135 lbs. of sand, and 180 lbs. of gravel

39. A tank that is 5/8 full is holding 200 gallons of gasoline. The amount of gasoline this tank can hold when filled to capacity is
   A. 270 gals.   B. 320 gals.   C. 360 gals.   D. 410 gals.

40.

The shaded portion of the above drawing represents an icy walk surrounding a building. If it takes 1 lb. of rock salt to clear ice from every 100 square feet of walk, how many pounds of rock salt would be needed to clear the entire walk?
   A. 55   B. 60   C. 120   D. 175

KEY (CORRECT ANSWERS)

1. C	11. C	21. D	31. B
2. A	12. D	22. C	32. B
3. A	13. A	23. B	33. C
4. B	14. A	24. C	34. A
5. D	15. B	25. B	35. D
6. C	16. C	26. C	36. B
7. C	17. B	27. A	37. C
8. B	18. A	28. C	38. D
9. D	19. D	29. D	39. B
10. C	20. D	30. B	40. A

EXAMINATION SECTION
TEST 1

DIRECTIONS: Each question or incomplete statement is followed by several suggested answers or completions. Select the one that BEST answers the question or completes the statement. *PRINT THE LETTER OF THE CORRECT ANSWER IN THE SPACE AT THE RIGHT.*

1. A herbicide is a chemical PRIMARILY used as a(n) 1.___
    A. disinfectant   B. fertilizer
    C. insect killer D. weed killer

2. Established plants that continue to blossom year after year without reseeding are GENERALLY known as 2.___
    A. annuals   B. parasites
    C. perennials D. symbiotics

3. A ferrous sulfate solution is sometimes used to treat shrubs or trees that have a deficiency of 3.___
    A. boron   B. copper   C. iron   D. zinc

4. A tree is described as deciduous. This means PRIMARILY that it 4.___
    A. bears nuts instead of fruit
    B. has been pruned recently
    C. usually grows in swampy ground
    D. loses its leaves in the fall

5. If you are told that a container holds a 20-7-7 fertilizer, it is MOST likely that twenty percent of this fertilizer is 5.___
    A. nitrogen   B. oxygen
    C. phosphoric acid D. potash

6. The landscape drawings for a school indicate the planting of *Acer platanoides* at a certain location on the grounds. Acer platanoides is a type of 6.___
    A. privet hedge B. rose bush
    C. maple tree   D. tulip bed

7. The commercial fertilizer *5-10-5* refers to 5% _____, 10% _____, 5% _____. 7.___
    A. nitrogen; phosphoric acid; potash
    B. rotted manure; calcium chloride; bone meal
    C. soda; tobacco dust; bone meal
    D. tobacco dust; rotted manure; sulphur

8. The slope or slant of a soil line is ¼" per foot. If this drainage line is 50' long, the difference in elevation from one end to the other is, in feet, MOST NEARLY 8.___
    A. 0.55   B. 1.04   C. 2.08   D. 12.5

9. The BEST method to use in watering trees and shrubs is to use
   A. jet-type velocity at roots
   B. hose with fine nozzle spray once a week and done well
   C. a hose only when needed to soak roots
   D. rotating single jet sprinkler

10. Little white insects that look like small shrimps and feed on the roots of grass are called
    A. grubs   B. ricks
    C. praying mantis   D. crabs

11. A term used to indicate a lawn chemical weed killer is
    A. germicide   B. emulsified
    C. herbicide   D. vitrified

12. The area of a lawn which is 58 feet wide by 96 feet long is MOST NEARLY _____ square feet.
    A. 5000   B. 5500   C. 6000   D. 6500

13. If it is not possible to plant new shrubs immediately upon delivery in the spring, they should be stored in a(n)
    A. sheltered outdoor area   B. unsheltered outdoor area
    C. boiler room   D. warm place indoors

14. Peat moss is GENERALLY used for its
    A. food value
    B. nitrogen
    C. alkalinity
    D. moisture retaining quality

15. A checklist of outdoor tasks which should be performed in March and April should NOT include
    A. fertilizing lawn areas
    B. applying dormant spray
    C. cleaning window wells
    D. spraying broad-leaved weeds

16. Lawns should be mowed when the grass has attained a height of _____ inch(es) with the mower set at _____ inch(es).
    A. 4; 3   B. 3; 2   C. 2; 1   D. 1; ½

17. The common name for a tree called Quercus Alba is
    A. pine   B. maple   C. oak   D. cedar

18. A tree which is considered to be suitable for street curb planting should
    A. grow rapidly
    B. have colorful foliage
    C. be an evergreen
    D. be straight and symmetrical

19. The component of fertilizers which aids in keeping grass   19.____
    from turning brown in the summer time is
       A. limestone   B. calcium   C. chlordane   D. nitrogen

20. A rectangular plot is 30 feet wide by 60 feet long.   20.____
    The length of the diagonal, in feet, is MOST NEARLY
       A. 68   B. 67   C. 66   D. 65

21. Pruning of street trees is the responsibility of the   21.____
       A. homeowners
       B. lighting company
       C. Department of Parks or Highways
       D. sanitation department

22. Of the following, the one that is MOST likely to be used   22.____
    in landscaping work as ground cover is
       A. Barberry   B. Forsythia
       C. Pachysandra   D. Viburnum

23. To help plants survive the shock of transplanting, in   23.____
    most cases, it is BEST to
       A. spray them with insecticide every day for a week
       B. cover the foliage with burlap for a day or two
       C. shade them from the sun for a week or two
       D. prune them every day for a week or two

24. Garden soil which has a pH reading of 6.0 is said to be   24.____
       A. neutral   B. slightly acid
       C. slightly alkaline   D. strongly acid

25. Summer blooming flower bulbs should be stored in a _____   25.____
    place.
       A. warm, dry   B. warm, moist
       C. cool, moist   D. cool, dry

26. The one of the following procedures which is NOT   26.____
    recommended for growing turfgrass in shaded areas is to
       A. fertilize more frequently than normal
       B. water deeply and frequently
       C. compact the soil as much as possible
       D. prune shallow tree roots as much as possible

27. Hedges should be trimmed so that the top is _____ than the   27.____
    bottom with the solid leaf growth starting _____ the
    ground.
       A. *narrower*; about eighteen inches above
       B. *narrower*; as close as possible to
       C. *wider*; about eighteen inches above
       D. *wider*; as close as possible to

28. When cutting a branch off a tree, it is DESIRABLE to   28.____
    undercut because it will
       A. prevent the weight of the branch from tearing off
          bark and wood below the cut
       B. make the tree grow stronger and straighter

C. let the saw work smoother and easier
D. make it easier to cut up the limb

29. The MAIN reason for applying lime to soil is to control its
    A. aridity   B. fertilization
    C. acidity   D. porosity

30. The GREATEST danger to a tree from a large unprotected wound is that
    A. birds may build a nest in it
    B. the tree may bleed to death
    C. the wound may become infected
    D. it is open to the elements

31. The fertilizer that is used for the care of trees should have a HIGH content of
    A. DDT   B. nitrogen   C. sulphur   D. carbon

32. The area of the plot shown at the right is _____ square feet.
    A. 25,300
    B. 26,700
    C. 28,100
    D. 30,500

33. Before pruning a tree, the FIRST step should be to determine
    A. if there is insect infestation
    B. the general health of the tree
    C. the desired results
    D. amount of excess foliage

34. Under normal conditions during the growing season, lawns should receive a good saturation of water with a spray
    A. once a day   B. once a week
    C. once a month   D. twice a month

35. A pH value of 4 would indicate a(n) _____ solution.
    A. acid   B. neutral   C. alkaline   D. dry

KEY (CORRECT ANSWERS)

1. D	11. C	21. C	31. B
2. C	12. B	22. C	32. C
3. C	13. A	23. C	33. C
4. D	14. D	24. B	34. B
5. A	15. D	25. D	35. A
6. C	16. B	26. C	
7. A	17. C	27. B	
8. B	18. D	28. A	
9. C	19. D	29. C	
10. A	20. B	30. C	

EXAMINATION SECTION
TEST 1

DIRECTIONS: Each question or incomplete statement is followed by several suggested answers or completions. Select the one that BEST answers the question or completes the statement. *PRINT THE LETTER OF THE CORRECT ANSWER IN THE SPACE AT THE RIGHT.*

1. Before starting any lawn mowing, the distance between the blade and a flat surface should be measured with a ruler. This distance should be such that the cut of the grass above the ground is _____ inch(es).   1.___
   A. 1   B. 1½   C. 2   D. 3

2. Strainers in a number 6 fuel oil system should be checked once a   2.___
   A. day   B. week   C. month   D. year

3. The spinning cup on a rotary cup oil burner should be cleaned   3.___
   A. once a day   B. once a week
   C. every 2 weeks   D. once a month

4. Terrazzo floors should be cleaned daily with a   4.___
   A. damp mop using clear water
   B. damp mop using a strong alkaline solution
   C. damp mop using a mild acid solution
   D. dust mop treated with vegetable oil

5. New installations of vinyl-asbestos floors should   5.___
   A. never be machine scrubbed
   B. be dry buffed weekly
   C. be swept daily, using an oily compound
   D. never be swept with treated dust mops

6. Standpipe fire hose shall be inspected   6.___
   A. monthly   B. quarterly
   C. semi-annually   D. annually

7. All portable fire extinguishers shall be inspected once   7.___
   A. a year   B. a month
   C. a week   D. every 3 months

8. Soda-acid and foam-type fire extinguishers shall be discharged and recharged AT LEAST once   8.___
   A. each year   B. every 2 years
   C. every 6 months   D. each month

9. Elevator *safeties* under the car shall be tested once each   9.___
   A. day   B. week   C. month   D. quarter

10. Key-type fire alarms in public school buildings shall be tested
   A. daily   B. weekly   C. monthly   D. quarterly

11. Combustion efficiency can be determined from an appropriate chart used in conjunction with
   A. steam temperature and steam pressure
   B. flue gas temperature and percentage of CO_2
   C. flue gas temperature and fuel heating value
   D. oil temperature and steam pressure

12. In the combustion of common fuels, the MAJOR boiler heat loss is due to
   A. incomplete combustion
   B. moisture in the fuel
   C. heat radiation
   D. heat lost in the flue gases

13. The MOST important reason for blowing down a boiler water column and gauge glass is to
   A. prevent the gauge glass level from rising too high
   B. relieve stresses in the gauge glass
   C. insure a true water level reading
   D. insure a true pressure gauge reading

14. The secondary voltage of a transformer used for ignition in a fuel oil burner has a range of MOST NEARLY _____ volts to _____ volts.
   A. 120; 240
   B. 440; 660
   C. 660; 1,200
   D. 5,000; 15,000

15. Assume that during the month of April there were 3 days with an average outdoor temperature of 30°F, 7 days with 40°F, 10 days with 50°F, 3 days with 60°F, and 7 days with 65°F.
   The number of degree days for the month was
   A. 330   B. 445   C. 595   D. 1,150

16. The pH of boiler feedwater is USUALLY maintained within the range of
   A. 4 to 5   B. 6 to 7   C. 10 to 12   D. 13 to 14

17. The admission of steam to the coils of a domestic hot water supply tank is regulated by a(n)
   A. pressure regulating valve
   B. immersion type temperature gauge
   C. check valve
   D. thermostatic control valve

18. The device which senses primary air failure in a rotary cup oil burner is USUALLY called a(n)
   A. vaporstate
   B. anemometer
   C. venturi
   D. pressure gauge

19. The device which starts and stops the flow of oil into an automatic rotary cup oil burner is USUALLY called a(n) _____ valve.
    A. magnetic oil
    B. oil metering
    C. oil check
    D. relief

20. A vacuum breaker, used on a steam heated domestic hot water tank, is USUALLY connected to the
    A. circulating pump
    B. tank wall
    C. aquastat
    D. steam coil flange

21. A vacuum pump in a low pressure steam heating system which is equipped with a float switch, a vacuum switch, a magnetic starter, and a selector switch, can be operated on
    A. float, vacuum, or automatic
    B. float, vacuum, or continuous
    C. vacuum, automatic, or continuous
    D. float, automatic, or continuous

22. If the temperature of the condensate returning to the vacuum pump in a low pressure steam vacuum heating system is above 180°F, the trouble may be caused by
    A. faulty radiator traps
    B. room thermostats being set too high
    C. uninsulated return lines
    D. too many radiators being shut off

23. A feedwater regulator operates to
    A. shut down the burner when the water is low
    B. maintain the water in the boiler at a predetermined level
    C. drain the water in the boiler
    D. regulate the temperature of the feedwater

24. An automatically fired steam boiler is equipped with an automatic low water cut-off.
    The low water cut-off is USUALLY actuated by
    A. steam pressure
    B. fuel pressure
    C. float action
    D. water temperature

25. Low pressure steam or an electric heater is USUALLY required for heating _____ fuel oil.
    A. #1
    B. #2
    C. #4
    D. #6

KEY (CORRECT ANSWERS)

1. C	6. B	11. B	16. C	21. D
2. A	7. B	12. D	17. D	22. A
3. A	8. A	13. C	18. A	23. B
4. A	9. C	14. D	19. A	24. C
5. B	10. A	15. B	20. D	25. D

TEST 2

DIRECTIONS: Each question or incomplete statement is followed by several suggested answers or completions. Select the one that BEST answers the question or completes the statement. *PRINT THE LETTER OF THE CORRECT ANSWER IN THE SPACE AT THE RIGHT.*

1. A compound gauge is calibrated to read
   A. pressure *only*
   B. vacuum *only*
   C. vacuum and pressure
   D. temperature and humidity

1.___

2. In a mechanical pressure-atomizing type oil burner, the oil is automized by using an automizing tip and
   A. steam pressure
   B. pump pressure
   C. compressed air
   D. a spinning cup

2.___

3. A good over-the-fire draft in a natural draft furnace should be *approximately* _____ inch(es) of water _____.
   A. 5.0; positive pressure
   B. 0.05; positive pressure
   C. 0.05; vacuum
   D. 5.0; vacuum

3.___

4. When it is necessary to add chemicals to a heating boiler, it should be done
   A. immediately after boiler blowdown
   B. after the boiler has been cleaned internally of sludge, scale, and other foreign matter
   C. at periods when condensate flow to the boiler is small
   D. at a time when there is a heavy flow of condensate to the boiler

4.___

5. The modutrol motor on a rotary cup oil burner burning #6 fuel oil automatically operates the primary air damper,
   A. secondary air damper, and oil metering valve
   B. secondary air damper, and magnetic oil valve
   C. oil metering valve, and magnetic oil valve
   D. and magnetic oil valve

5.___

6. The manual-reset pressuretrol is classified as a
   A. Safety and Operating Control
   B. Limit and Operating Control
   C. Limit and Safety Control
   D. Limit, Operating, and Safety Control

6.___

7. Sodium sulphite is added to boiler feedwater to
   A. avoid caustic embrittlement
   B. increase the pH value
   C. reduce the tendency of foaming in the steam drum
   D. remove dissolved oxygen

7.___

8. Neat cement is a mixture of cement,
   A. putty, and water
   B. and water
   C. lime, and water
   D. salt, and water

9. In a concrete mix of 1:2:4, the 2 refers to the amount of
   A. sand   B. cement   C. stone   D. water

10. The word *natatorium* means MOST NEARLY a(n)
    A. auditorium
    B. playroom
    C. gymnasium
    D. indoor swimming pool

11. Plated metal surfaces which are protected by a thin coat of clear lacquer should be cleaned with a(n)
    A. abrasive compound
    B. liquid polish
    C. mild soap solution
    D. lemon oil solution

12. Wet mop filler replacements are ordered by
    A. length
    B. weight
    C. number of strands
    D. trade number

13. The BEST way to determine the value of a cleaning material is by
    A. performance testing
    B. manufacturer's literature
    C. written specifications
    D. interviews with manufacturer's salesman

14. Instructions on a container of cleaning compound state: *Mix one pound of compound in 5 gallons of water.* Using these instructions, the amount of compound which should be added to 15 quarts of water is MOST NEARLY _____ ounces.
    A. 3   B. 8   C. 12   D. 48

15. The MOST usual cause of paint blisters is
    A. too much oil in the paint
    B. moisture under the paint coat
    C. a heavy coat of paint
    D. improper drying of paint

16. The floor that should NOT be machine scrubbed is a(n)
    A. lobby
    B. lunchroom
    C. gymnasium
    D. auditorium aisle

17. Pick-up sweeping in a public building is the occasional removal of the more conspicuous loose dirt from corridors and lobbies.
    This type of sweeping should be done
    A. after scrubbing or waving of floors
    B. with the aid of a sweeping compound
    C. at night after school hours
    D. during regular school hours

18. According to recommended practice, when a steam boiler is taken out of service for a long period of time, the boiler drums should FIRST be
    A. drained completely while the water is hot (above 212°F)
    B. drained completely after the water has been cooled down to 180°F
    C. filled completely without draining
    D. filled to the level of the top try cock

19. The prevention and control of vermin and rodents in a building is PRIMARILY a matter of
    A. maintaining good housekeeping on a continuous basis
    B. periodic use of an exterminator's service
    C. calling in the exterminator when necessary
    D. cleaning the building thoroughly during school vacation

20. If it is not possible to plant new shrubs immediately upon delivery in the spring, they should be stored in a(n)
    A. sheltered outdoor area   B. unsheltered outdoor area
    C. boiler room   D. warm place indoors

21. Peat moss is *generally* used for its
    A. food value   B. nitrogen
    C. alkalinity   D. moisture retaining quality

22. The legal minimum age of employees engaged for cleaning windows in the state is _____ years.
    A. 16   B. 17   C. 18   D. 21

23. The MAIN classification of lumber used for construction purposes is known as _____ lumber.
    A. industrial   B. commercial
    C. finish   D. yard

24. Specifications concerning window cleaners' anchors and safety belts must be in compliance with the rules and regulations outlined in the
    A. state labor law and board of standards and appeals
    B. city building code
    C. fire department safety manual
    D. national protection code

25. Pruning of street trees is the responsibility of the
    A. custodian-engineer   B. board of education
    C. department of parks   D. borough president's office

KEY (CORRECT ANSWERS)

1. C	6. C	11. C	16. C	21. D
2. B	7. D	12. B	17. D	22. C
3. C	8. B	13. A	18. B	23. D
4. D	9. A	14. C	19. A	24. A
5. A	10. D	15. B	20. A	25. C

PHILOSOPHY, PRINCIPLES, PRACTICES, AND TECHNICS
OF
SUPERVISION, ADMINISTRATION, MANAGEMENT, AND ORGANIZATION

CONTENTS

	Page
I. MEANING OF SUPERVISION	1
II. THE OLD AND THE NEW SUPERVISION	1
III. THE EIGHT (8) BASIC PRINCIPLES OF THE NEW SUPERVISION	1
1. Principle of Responsibility	1
2. Principle of Authority	1
3. Principle of Self-Growth	1
4. Principle of Individual Worth	2
5. Principle of Creative Leadership	2
6. Principle of Success and Failure	2
7. Principle of Science	2
8. Principle of Cooperation	2
IV. WHAT IS ADMINISTRATION?	3
1. Practices Commonly Classed as "Supervisory"	3
2. Practices Commonly Classed as "Administrative"	3
3. Practices Classified as Both "Supervisory" and "Administrative"	3
V. RESPONSIBILITIES OF THE SUPERVISOR	3
VI. COMPETENCIES OF THE SUPERVISOR	4
VII. THE PROFESSIONAL SUPERVISOR-EMPLOYEE RELATIONSHIP	4
VIII. MINI-TEXT IN SUPERVISION, ADMINISTRATION, MANAGEMENT, AND ORGANIZATION	5
A. Brief Highlights	
1. Levels of Management	5
2. What the Supervisor Must Learn	5
3. A Definition of Supervision	6
4. Elements of the Team Concept	6
5. Principles of Organization	6
6. The Four Important Parts of Every Job	6
7. Principles of Delegation	6
8. Principles of Effective Communications	6
9. Principles of Work Improvement	6
10. Areas of Job Improvement	7
11. Seven Key Points in Making Improvements	7
12. Corrective Techniques of Job Improvement	7
13. A Planning Checklist	7
14. Five Characteristics of Good Directions	7
15. Types of Directions	8
16. Controls	8
17. Orienting the New Employee	8
18. Checklist for Orienting New Employees	8
19. Principles of Learning	8
20. Causes of Poor Performance	8
21. Four Major Steps in On-The-Job Instructions	8

CONTENTS (cont'd)

	Page
22. Employees Want Five Things	9
23. Some Don'ts in Regard to Praise	9
24. How to Gain Your Workers' Confidence	9
25. Sources of Employee Problems	9
26. The Supervisor's Key to Discipline	9
27. Five Important Processes of Management	10
28. When the Supervisor Fails to Plan	10
29. Fourteen General Principles of Management	10
30. Change	10
B. Brief Topical Summaries	11
I. Who/What is the Supervisor?	11
II. The Sociology of Work	11
III. Principles and Practices of Supervision	11
IV. Dynamic Leadership	12
V. Processes for Solving Problems	12
VI. Training for Results	13
VII. Health, Safety, and Accident Prevention	13
VIII. Equal Employment Opportunity	13
IX. Improving Communications	14
X. Self-Development	14
XI. Teaching and Training	14
A. The Teaching Process	14
1. Preparation	15
2. Presentation	15
3. Summary	15
4. Application	15
5. Evaluation	15
B. Teaching Methods	15
1. Lecture	16
2. Discussion	16
3. Demonstration	16
4. Performance	16
5. Which Method to Use	16

PHILOSOPHY, PRINCIPLES, PRACTICES, AND TECHNICS
OF
SUPERVISION, ADMINISTRATION, MANAGEMENT, AND ORGANIZATION

I. MEANING OF SUPERVISION

The extension of the democratic philosophy has been accompanied by an extension in the scope of supervision. Modern leaders and supervisors no longer think of supervision in the narrow sense of being confined chiefly to visiting employees, supplying materials, or rating the staff. They regard supervision as being intimately related to all the concerned agencies of society, they speak of the supervisor's function in terms of "growth", rather than the "improvement," of employees

This modern concept of supervision may be defined as follows:

Supervision is leadership and the development of leadership within groups which are cooperatively engaged in inspection, research, training, guidance and evaluation.

II. THE OLD AND THE NEW SUPERVISION

TRADITIONAL	*MODERN*
1. Inspection	1. Study and analysis
2. Focused on the employee	2. Focused on aims, materials, methods, supervisors, employees, environment
3. Visitation	3. Demonstrations, intervisitation, workshops, directed reading, bulletins, etc.
4. Random and haphazard	4. Definitely organized and planned (scientific)
5. Imposed and authoritarian	5. Cooperative and democratic
6. One person usually	6. Many persons involved (creative)

III. THE EIGHT (8) BASIC PRINCIPLES OF THE NEW SUPERVISION

1. *PRINCIPLE OF RESPONSIBILITY*

    Authority to act and responsibility for acting must be joined.
    a. If you give responsibility, give authority.
    b. Define employee duties clearly.
    c. Protect employees from criticism by others.
    d. Recognize the rights as well as obligations of employees.
    e. Achieve the aims of a democratic society insofar as it is possible within the area of your work.
    f. Establish a situation favorable to training and learning.
    g. Accept ultimate responsibility for everything done in your section, unit, office, division, department.
    h. Good administration and good supervision are inseparable.

2. *PRINCIPLE OF AUTHORITY*

    The success of the supervisor is measured by the extent to which the power of authority is not used.
    a. Exercise simplicity and informality in supervision.
    b. Use the simplest machinery of supervision.
    c. If it is good for the organization as a whole, it is probably justified.
    d. Seldom be arbitrary or authoritative.
    e. Do not base your work on the power of position or of personality.
    f. Permit and encourage the free expression of opinions.

3. *PRINCIPLE OF SELF-GROWTH*

    The success of the supervisor is measured by the extent to which, and the speed with which, he is no longer needed.
    a. Base criticism on principles, not on specifics.
    b. Point out higher activities to employees.

c. Train for self-thinking by employees, to meet new situations.
   d. Stimulate initiative, self-reliance and individual responsibility.
   e. Concentrate on stimulating the growth of employees rather than on removing defects.
4. *PRINCIPLE OF INDIVIDUAL WORTH*
   Respect for the individual is a paramount consideration in supervision.
   a. Be human and sympathetic in dealing with employees.
   b. Don't nag about things to be done.
   c. Recognize the individual differences among employees and seek opportunities to permit best expression of each personality.
5. *PRINCIPLE OF CREATIVE LEADERSHIP*
   The best supervision is that which is not apparent to the employee.
   a. Stimulate, don't drive employees to creative action.
   b. Emphasize doing good things.
   c. Encourage employees to do what they do best.
   d. Do not be too greatly concerned with details of subject or method.
   e. Do not be concerned exclusively with immediate problems and activities.
   f. Reveal higher activities and make them both desired and maximally possible.
   g. Determine procedures in the light of each situation but see that these are derived from a sound basic philosophy.
   h. Aid, inspire and lead so as to liberate the creative spirit latent in all good employees.
6. *PRINCIPLE OF SUCCESS AND FAILURE*
   There are no unsuccessful employees, only unsuccessful supervisors who have failed to give proper leadership.
   a. Adapt suggestions to the capacities, attitudes, and prejudices of employees.
   b. Be gradual, be progressive, be persistent.
   c. Help the employee find the general principle; have the employee apply his own problem to the general principle.
   d. Give adequate appreciation for good work and honest effort.
   e. Anticipate employee difficulties and help to prevent them.
   f. Encourage employees to do the desirable things they will do anyway.
   g. Judge your supervision by the results it secures.
7. *PRINCIPLE OF SCIENCE*
   Successful supervision is scientific, objective, and experimental. It is based on facts, not on prejudices.
   a. Be cumulative in results.
   b. Never divorce your suggestions from the goals of training.
   c. Don't be impatient of results.
   d. Keep all matters on a professional, not a personal level.
   e. Do not be concerned exclusively with immediate problems and activities.
   f. Use objective means of determining achievement and rating where possible.
8. *PRINCIPLE OF COOPERATION*
   Supervision is a cooperative enterprise between supervisor and employee.
   a. Begin with conditions as they are.
   b. Ask opinions of all involved when formulating policies.

      c. Organization is as good as its weakest link.
      d. Let employees help to determine policies and department programs.
      e. Be approachable and accessible - physically and mentally.
      f. Develop pleasant social relationships.

V. WHAT IS ADMINISTRATION?

Administration is concerned with providing the environment, the material facilities, and the operational procedures that will promote the maximum growth and development of supervisors and employees. (Organization is an aspect, and a concomitant, of administration.)

There is no sharp line of demarcation between supervision and administration; these functions are intimately interrelated and, often, overlapping. They are complementary activities.

1. *PRACTICES COMMONLY CLASSED AS "SUPERVISORY"*
    a. Conducting employees conferences
    b. Visiting sections, units, offices, divisions, departments
    c. Arranging for demonstrations
    d. Examining plans
    e. Suggesting professional reading
    f. Interpreting bulletins
    g. Recommending in-service training courses
    h. Encouraging experimentation
    i. Appraising employee morale
    j. Providing for intervisitation
2. *PRACTICES COMMONLY CLASSIFIED AS "ADMINISTRATIVE"*
    a. Management of the office
    b. Arrangement of schedules for extra duties
    c. Assignment of rooms or areas
    d. Distribution of supplies
    e. Keeping records and reports
    f. Care of audio-visual materials
    g. Keeping inventory records
    h. Checking record cards and books
    i. Programming special activities
    j. Checking on the attendance and punctuality of employees
3. *PRACTICES COMMONLY CLASSIFIED AS BOTH "SUPERVISORY" AND "ADMINISTRATIVE"*
    a. Program construction
    b. Testing or evaluating outcomes
    c. Personnel accounting
    d. Ordering instructional materials

V. RESPONSIBILITIES OF THE SUPERVISOR

A person employed in a supervisory capacity must constantly be able to improve his own efficiency and ability. He represents the employer to the employees and only continuous self-examination can make him a capable supervisor.

Leadership and training are the supervisor's responsibility. An efficient working unit is one in which the employees work with the supervisor. It is his job to bring out the best in his employees. He must always be relaxed, courteous and calm in his association with his employees. Their feelings are important, and a harsh attitude does not develop the most efficient employees.

VI. COMPETENCIES OF THE SUPERVISOR
1. Complete knowledge of the duties and responsibilities of his position.
2. To be able to organize a job, plan ahead and carry through.
3. To have self-confidence and initiative.
4. To be able to handle the unexpected situation and make quick decisions.
5. To be able to properly train subordinates in the positions they are best suited for.
6. To be able to keep good human relations among his subordinates.
7. To be able to keep good human relations between his subordinate and himself and to earn their respect and trust.

VII. THE PROFESSIONAL SUPERVISOR-EMPLOYEE RELATIONSHIP

There are two kinds of efficiency: one kind is only apparent and is produced in organizations through the exercise of mere discipline; this is but a simulation of the second, or true, efficiency which springs from spontaneous cooperation. If you are a manager, no matter how great or small your responsibility, it is your job, in the final analysis, to create and develop this involuntary cooperation among the people whom you supervise. For, no matter how powerful a combination of money, machines, and materials a company may have, this is a dead and sterile thing without a team of willing, thinking and articulate people to guide it.

The following 21 points are presented as indicative of the exemplabasic relationship that should exist between supervisor and employee

1. Each person wants to be liked and respected by his fellow employee and wants to be treated with consideration and respect by hi superior.
2. The most competent employee will make an error. However, in a unit where good relations exist between the supervisor and his employees, tenseness and fear do not exist. Thus, errors are not hidden or covered up and the efficiency of a unit is not impaired.
3. Subordinates resent rules, regulations, or orders that are unreasonable or unexplained.
4. Subordinates are quick to resent unfairness, harshness, injustices and favoritism.
5. An employee will accept responsibility if he knows that he will be complimented for a job well done, and not too harshly chastized for failure; that his supervisor will check the cause of the failure, and, if it was the supervisor's fault, he will assume the blame therefor. If it was the employee's fault, his supervisor will explain the correct method or means of handling the responsibility.
6. An employee wants to receive credit for a suggestion he has made, that is used. If a suggestion cannot be used, the employee is entitled to an explanation. The supervisor should not say "no" and close the subject.
7. Fear and worry slow up a worker's ability. Poor working environment can impair his physical and mental health. A good supervisor avoids forceful methods, threats and arguments to get a job done.
8. A forceful supervisor is able to train his employees individually and as a team, and is able to motivate them in the proper channels.

9. A mature supervisor is able to properly evaluate his subordinates and to keep them happy and satisfied.
10. A sensitive supervisor will never patronize his subordinates.
11. A worthy supervisor will respect his employees' confidences.
12. Definite and clear-cut responsibilities should be assigned to each executive.
13. Responsibility should always be coupled with corresponding authority.
14. No change should be made in the scope or responsibilities of a position without a definite understanding to that effect on the part of all persons concerned.
15. No executive or employee, occupying a single position in the organization, should be subject to definite orders from more than one source.
16. Orders should never be given to subordinates over the head of a responsible executive. Rather than do this, the officer in question should be supplanted.
17. Criticisms of subordinates should, whever possible, be made privately, and in no case should a subordinate be criticized in the presence of executives or employees of equal or lower rank.
18. No dispute or difference between executives or employees as to authority or responsibilities should be considered too trivial for prompt and careful adjudication.
19. Promotions, wage changes, and disciplinary action should always be approved by the executive immediately superior to the one directly responsible.
20. No executive or employee should ever be required, or expected, to be at the same time an assistant to, and critic of, another.
21. Any executive whose work is subject to regular inspection should, whever practicable, be given the assistance and facilities necessary to enable him to maintain an independent check of the quality of his work.

III. MINI-TEXT IN SUPERVISION, ADMINISTRATION, MANAGEMENT, AND ORGANIZATION
A. BRIEF HIGHLIGHTS
Listed concisely and sequentially are major headings and important data in the field for quick recall and review.

1. *LEVELS OF MANAGEMENT*

   Any organization of some size has several levels of management. In terms of a ladder the levels are:

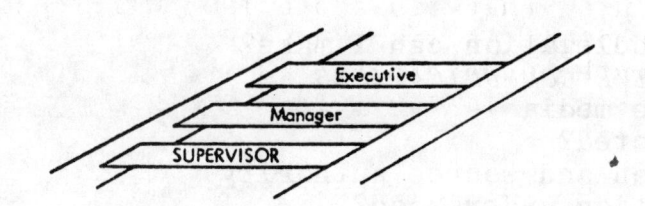

   ```
   Executive
   Manager
   SUPERVISOR
   ```

   The first level is very important because it is the beginning point of management leadership.

2. *WHAT THE SUPERVISOR MUST LEARN*

   A supervisor must learn to:
   (1) Deal with people and their differences
   (2) Get the job done through people
   (3) Recognize the problems when they exist
   (4) Overcome obstacles to good performance
   (5) Evaluate the performance of people
   (6) Check his own performance in terms of accomplishment

3. *A DEFINITION OF SUPERVISOR*

   The term supervisor means any individual having authority, in the interests of the employer, to hire, transfer, suspend, lay-off, recall, promote, discharge, assign, reward, or discipline other employees... or responsibility to direct them, or to adjust their grievances, or effectively to recommend such action, if, in connection with the foregoing, exercise of such authority is not of a merely routine or clerical nature but requires the use of independent judgment.

4. *ELEMENTS OF THE TEAM CONCEPT*

   What is involved in teamwork? The component parts are:
   - (1) Members
   - (2) A leader
   - (3) Goals
   - (4) Plans
   - (5) Cooperation
   - (6) Spirit

5. *PRINCIPLES OF ORGANIZATION*
   - (1) A team member must know what his job is
   - (2) Be sure that the nature and scope of a job are understood
   - (3) Authority and responsibility should be carefully spelled out
   - (4) A supervisor should be permitted to make the maximum number of decisions affecting his employees
   - (5) Employees should report to only one supervisor
   - (6) A supervisor should direct only as many employees as he can handle effectively
   - (7) An organization plan should be flexible
   - (8) Inspection and performance of work should be separate
   - (9) Organizational problems should receive immediate attention
   - (10) Assign work in line with ability and experience

6. *THE FOUR IMPORTANT PARTS OF EVERY JOB*
   - (1) Inherent in every job is the *accountability* for results
   - (2) A second set of factors in every job are *responsibilities*
   - (3) Along with duties and responsibilities one must have the *authority* to act within certain limits without obtaining permission to proceed
   - (4) No job exists in a vacuum. The supervisor is surrounded by key *relationships*

7. *PRINCIPLES OF DELEGATION*

   Where work is delegated for the first time, the supervisor should think in terms of these questions:
   - (1) Who is best qualified to do this?
   - (2) Can an employee improve his abilities by doing this?
   - (3) How long should an employee spend on this?
   - (4) Are there any special problems for which he will need guidance?
   - (5) How broad a delegation can I make?

8. *PRINCIPLES OF EFFECTIVE COMMUNICATIONS*
   - (1) Determine the media
   - (2) To whom directed?
   - (3) Identification and source authority
   - (4) Is communication understood?

9. *PRINCIPLES OF WORK IMPROVEMENT*
   - (1) Most people usually do only the work which is assigned to them
   - (2) Workers are likely to fit assigned work into the time available to perform it
   - (3) A good workload usually stimulates output
   - (4) People usually do their best work when they know that results will be reviewed or inspected

        (5) Employees usually feel that someone else is responsible for
            conditions of work, workplace layout, job methods, type of
            tools and equipment, and other such factors
        (6) Employees are usually defensive about their job security
        (7) Employees have natural resistance to change
        (8) Employees can support or destroy a supervisor
        (9) A supervisor usually earns the respect of his people through
            his personal example of diligence and efficiency
10. *AREAS OF JOB IMPROVEMENT*
    The *areas* of job improvement are quite numerous, but the most common ones which a supervisor can identify and utilize are:
        (1) Departmental layout   (5) Work methods
        (2) Flow of work   (6) Materials handling
        (3) Workplace layout   (7) Utilization
        (4) Utilization of manpower (8) Motion economy
11. *SEVEN KEY POINTS IN MAKING IMPROVEMENTS*
        (1) Select the job to be improved
        (2) Study how it is being done now
        (3) Question the present method
        (4) Determine actions to be taken
        (5) Chart proposed method
        (6) Get approval and apply
        (7) Solicit worker participation
12. *CORRECTIVE TECHNIQUES OF JOB IMPROVEMENT*

Specific Problems	*General Problems*	*Corrective Technique*
(1) Size of workload	(1) Departmental layout	(1) Study with scale model
(2) Inability to meet schedules	(2) Flow of work	(2) Flow chart study
(3) Strain and fatigue	(3) Workplan layout	(3) Motion analysis
(4) Improper use of men and skills	(4) Utilization of manpower	(4) Comparison of units produced to standard allowances
(5) Waste, poor quality, unsafe conditions	(5) Work methods	(5) Methods analysis
(6) Bottleneck conditions that hinder output	(6) Materials handling	(6) Flow chart and equipment study
(7) Poor utilization of equipment and machines	(7) Utilization of equipment	(7) Down time vs. running time
(8) Efficiency and productivity of labor	(8) Motion economy	(8) Motion analysis

13. *A PLANNING CHECKLIST*
        (1) Objectives   (8) Equipment
        (2) Controls   (9) Supplies and materials
        (3) Delegations   (10) Utilization of time
        (4) Communications   (11) Safety
        (5) Resources   (12) Money
        (6) Methods and procedures (13) Work
        (7) Manpower   (14) Timing of improvements
14. *FIVE CHARACTERISTICS OF GOOD DIRECTIONS*
    In order to get results, directions must be:
        (1) Possible of accomplishment   (4) Planned and complete
        (2) Agreeable with worker interests (5) Unmistakably clear
        (3) Related to mission

15. *TYPES OF DIRECTIONS*
    (1) Demands or direct orders   (3) Suggestion or implication
    (2) Requests   (4) Volunteering
16. *CONTROLS*
    A typical listing of the overall areas in which the supervisor should establish controls might be:
    (1) Manpower   (4) Quantity of work   (7) Money
    (2) Materials   (5) Time   (8) Methods
    (3) Quality of work (6) Space
17. *ORIENTING THE NEW EMPLOYEE*
    (1) Prepare for him   (3) Orientation for the job
    (2) Welcome the new employee (4) Follow-up
18. *CHECKLIST FOR ORIENTING NEW EMPLOYEES*
                                                          Yes No
    (1) Do your appreciate the feelings of new employees when they first report for work? ... ...
    (2) Are you aware of the fact that the new employee must make a big adjustment to his job? ... ...
    (3) Have you given him good reasons for liking the job and the organization? ... ...
    (4) Have you prepared for his first day on the job? ... ...
    (5) Did you welcome him cordially and make him feel needed? ... ...
    (6) Did you establish rapport with him so that he feels free to talk and discuss matters with you? ... ...
    (7) Did you explain his job to him and his relationship to you? ... ...
    (8) Does he know that his work will be evaluated periodically on a basis that is fair and objective? ... ...
    (9) Did you introduce him to his fellow workers in such a way that they are likely to accept him? ... ...
    (10) Does he know what employee benefits he will receive? ... ...
    (11) Does he understand the importance of being on the job and what to do if he must leave his duty station? ... ...
    (12) Has he been impressed with the importance of accident prevention and safe practice? ... ...
    (13) Does he generally know his way around the department? ... ...
    (14) Is he under the guidance of a sponsor who will teach the right ways of doing things? ... ...
    (15) Do you plan to follow-up so that he will continue to adjust successfully to his job? ... ...
19. *PRINCIPLES OF LEARNING*
    (1) Motivation (2) Demonstration or explanation
    (3) Practice
20. *CAUSES OF POOR PERFORMANCE*
    (1) Improper training for job   (6) Lack of standards of
    (2) Wrong tools   performance
    (3) Inadequate directions   (7) Wrong work habits
    (4) Lack of supervisory follow-up (8) Low morale
    (5) Poor communications   (9) Other
21. *FOUR MAJOR STEPS IN ON-THE-JOB INSTRUCTION*
    (1) Prepare the worker   (3) Tryout performance
    (2) Present the operation (4) Follow-up

22. *EMPLOYEES WANT FIVE THINGS*
    - (1) Security   (2) Opportunity   (3) Recognition
    - (4) Inclusion   (5) Expression
23. *SOME DON'TS IN REGARD TO PRAISE*
    - (1) Don't praise a person for something he hasn't done
    - (2) Don't praise a person unless you can be sincere
    - (3) Don't be sparing in praise just because your superior withholds it from you
    - (4) Don't let too much time elapse between good performance and recognition of it
24. *HOW TO GAIN YOUR WORKERS' CONFIDENCE*
    Methods of developing confidence include such things as:
    - (1) Knowing the interests, habits, hobbies of employees
    - (2) Admitting your own inadequacies
    - (3) Sharing and telling of confidence in others
    - (4) Supporting people when they are in trouble
    - (5) Delegating matters that can be well handled
    - (6) Being frank and straightforward about problems and working conditions
    - (7) Encouraging others to bring their problems to you
    - (8) Taking action on problems which impede worker progress
25. *SOURCES OF EMPLOYEE PROBLEMS*
    On-the-job causes might be such things as:
    - (1) A feeling that favoritism is exercised in assignments
    - (2) Assignment of overtime
    - (3) An undue amount of supervision
    - (4) Changing methods or systems
    - (5) Stealing of ideas or trade secrets
    - (6) Lack of interest in job
    - (7) Threat of reduction in force
    - (8) Ignorance or lack of communications
    - (9) Poor equipment
    - (10) Lack of knowing how supervisor feels toward employee
    - (11) Shift assignments

    Off-the-job problems might have to do with:
    - (1) Health   (2) Finances   (3) Housing   (4) Family
26. *THE SUPERVISOR'S KEY TO DISCIPLINE*
    There are several key points about discipline which the supervisor should keep in mind:
    - (1) Job discipline is one of the disciplines of life and is directed by the supervisor.
    - (2) It is more important to correct an employee fault than to fix blame for it.
    - (3) Employee performance is affected by problems both on the job and off.
    - (4) Sudden or abrupt changes in behavior can be indications of important employee problems.
    - (5) Problems should be dealt with as soon as possible after they are identified.
    - (6) The attitude of the supervisor may have more to do with solving problems than the techniques of problem solving.
    - (7) Correction of employee behavior should be resorted to only after the supervisor is sure that training or counseling will not be helpful
    - (8) Be sure to document your disciplinary actions.

         (9) Make sure that you are disciplining on the basis of facts
             rather than personal feelings.
        (10) Take each disciplinary step in order, being careful not to
             make snap judgments, or decisions based on impatience.
27. *FIVE IMPORTANT PROCESSES OF MANAGEMENT*
         (1) Planning   (2) Organizing   (3) Scheduling
         (4) Controlling   (5) Motivating
28. *WHEN THE SUPERVISOR FAILS TO PLAN*
         (1) Supervisor creates impression of not knowing his job
         (2) May lead to excessive overtime
         (3) Job runs itself-- supervisor lacks control
         (4) Deadlines and appointments missed
         (5) Parts of the work go undone
         (6) Work interrupted by emergencies
         (7) Sets a bad example
         (8) Uneven workload creates peaks and valleys
         (9) Too much time on minor details at expense of more important
             tasks
29. *FOURTEEN GENERAL PRINCIPLES OF MANAGEMENT*
         (1) Division of work   (8) Centralization
         (2) Authority and responsibility (9) Scalar chain
         (3) Discipline   (10) Order
         (4) Unity of command   (11) Equity
         (5) Unity of direction   (12) Stability of tenure of
         (6) Subordination of individual   personnel
             interest to general interest (13) Initiative
         (7) Remuneration of personnel   (14) Esprit de corps
30. *CHANGE*
    Bringing about change is perhaps attempted more often, and yet
less well understood, than anything else the supervisor does. How
do people generally react to change? (People tend to resist change
that is imposed upon them by other individuals or circumstances.)
    Change is characteristic of every situation. It is a part of every
real endeavor where the efforts of people are concerned.
    A. Why do people resist change?
         People may resist change because of:
             (1) Fear of the unknown
             (2) Implied criticism
             (3) Unpleasant experiences in the past
             (4) Fear of loss of status
             (5) Threat to the ego
             (6) Fear of loss of economic stability
    B. How can we best overcome the resistance to change?
         In initiating change, take these steps:
             (1) Get ready to sell
             (2) identify sources of help
             (3) Anticipate objections
             (4) Sell benefits
             (5) Listen in depth
             (6) Follow up

B. BRIEF TOPICAL SUMMARIES

I. WHO/WHAT IS THE SUPERVISOR?
1. The supervisor is often called the "highest level employee and the lowest level manager."
2. A supervisor is a member of both management and the work group. He acts as a bridge between the two.
3. Most problems in supervision are in the area of human relations, or people problems.
4. Employees expect: Respect, opportunity to learn and to advance, and a sense of belonging, and so forth.
5. Supervisors are responsible for directing people and organizing work. Planning is of paramount importance.
6. A position description is a set of duties and responsibilities inherent to a given position.
7. It is important to keep the position description up-to-date and to provide each employee with his own copy.

II. THE SOCIOLOGY OF WORK
1. People are alike in many ways; however each individual is unique.
2. The supervisor is challenged in getting to know employee differences. Acquiring skills in evaluating individuals is an asset.
3. Maintaining meaningful working relationships in the organization is of great importance.
4. The supervisor has an obligation to help individuals to develop to their fullest potential.
5. Job rotation on a planned basis helps to build versatility and to maintain interest and enthusiasm in work groups.
6. Cross training (job rotation) provides backup skills.
7. The supervisor can help reduce tension by maintaining a sense of humor, providing guidance to employees, and by making reasonable and timely decisions. Employees respond favorably to working under reasonably predictable circumstances.
8. Change is characteristic of all managerial behavior. The supervisor must adjust to changes in procedures, new methods, technological changes, and to a number of new and sometimes challenging situations.
9. To overcome the natural tendency for people to resist change, the supervisor should become more skillful in initiating change.

II. PRINCIPLES AND PRACTICES OF SUPERVISION
1. Employees should be required to answer to only one superior.
2. A supervisor can effectively direct only a limited number of employees, depending upon the complexity, variety, and proximity of the jobs involved.
3. The organizational chart presents the organization in graphic form. It reflects lines of authority and responsibility as well as interrelationships of units within the organization.
4. Distribution of work can be improved through an analysis using the "Work Distribution Chart."
5. The "Work Distribution Chart" reflects the division of work within a unit in understandable form.
6. When related tasks are given to an employee, he has a better chance of increasing his skills through training.
7. The individual who is given the responsibility for tasks must also be given the appropriate authority to insure adequate results.
8. The supervisor should delegate repetitive, routine work. Preparation of recurring reports, maintaining leave and attendance records are some examples.

9. Good discipline is essential to good task performance. Discipline is reflected in the actions of employees on the job in the absence of supervision.
10. Disciplinary action may have to be taken when the positive aspects of discipline have failed. Reprimand, warning, and suspension are examples of disciplinary action.
11. If a situation calls for a reprimand, be sure it is deserved and remember it is to be done in private.

IV. DYNAMIC LEADERSHIP
1. A style is a personal method or manner of exerting influence.
2. Authoritarian leaders often see themselves as the source of power and authority.
3. The democratic leader often perceives the group as the source of authority and power.
4. Supervisors tend to do better when using the pattern of leadership that is most natural for them.
5. Social scientists suggest that the effective supervisor use the leadership style that best fits the problem or circumstances involved.
6. All four styles -- telling, selling, consulting, joining -- have their place. Using one does not preclude using the other at another time.
7. The theory X point of view assumes that the average person dislikes work, will avoid it whenever possible, and must be coerced to achieve organizational objectives.
8. The theory Y point of view assumes that the average person considers work to be as natural as play, and, when the individual is committed, he requires little supervision or direction to accomplish desired objectives.
9. The leader's basic assumptions concerning human behavior and human nature affect his actions, decisions, and other managerial practices.
10. Dissatisfaction among employees is often present, but difficult to isolate. The supervisor should seek to weaken dissatisfaction by keeping promises, being sincere and considerate, keeping employees informed, and so forth.
11. Constructive suggestions should be encouraged during the natural progress of the work.

V. PROCESSES FOR SOLVING PROBLEMS
1. People find their daily tasks more meaningful and satisfying when they can improve them.
2. The causes of problems, or the key factors, are often hidden in the background. Ability to solve problems often involves the ability to isolate them from their backgrounds. There is some substance to the cliché that some persons "can't see the forest for the trees."
3. New procedures are often developed from old ones. Problems should be broken down into manageable parts. New ideas can be adapted from old ones.
4. People think differently in problem-solving situations. Using a logical, patterned approach is often useful. One approach found to be useful includes these steps:
   (a) Define the problem   (d) Weigh and decide
   (b) Establish objectives   (e) Take action
   (c) Get the facts   (f) Evaluate action

VI. TRAINING FOR RESULTS
1. Participants respond best when they feel training is important to them.
2. The supervisor has responsibility for the training and development of those who report to him.
3. When training is delegated to others, great care must be exercised to insure the trainer has knowledge, aptitude, and interest for his work as a trainer.
4. Training (learning) of some type goes on continually. The most successful supervisor makes certain the learning contributes in a productive manner to operational goals.
5. New employees are particularly susceptible to training. Older employees facing new job situations require specific training, as well as having need for development and growth opportunities.
6. Training needs require continuous monitoring.
7. The training officer of an agency is a professional with a responsibility to assist supervisors in solving training problems.
8. Many of the self-development steps important to the supervisor's own growth are equally important to the development of peers and subordinates. Knowledge of these is important when the supervisor consults with others on development and growth opportunities.

VII. HEALTH, SAFETY, AND ACCIDENT PREVENTION
1. Management-minded supervisors take appropriate measures to assist employees in maintaining health and in assuring safe practices in the work environment.
2. Effective safety training and practices help to avoid injury and accidents.
3. Safety should be a management goal. All infractions of safety which are observed should be corrected without exception.
4. Employees' safety attitude, training and instruction, provision of safe tools and equipment, supervision, and leadership are considered highly important factors which contribute to safety and which can be influenced directly by supervisors.
5. When accidents do occur they should be investigated promptly for very important reasons, including the fact that information which is gained can be used to prevent accidents in the future.

VIII. EQUAL EMPLOYMENT OPPORTUNITY
1. The supervisor should endeavor to treat all employees fairly, without regard to religion, race, sex, or national origin.
2. Groups tend to reflect the attitude of the leader. Prejudice can be detected even in very subtle form. Supervisors must strive to create a feeling of mutual respect and confidence in every employee.
3. Complete utilization of all human resources is a national goal. Equitable consideration should be accorded women in the work force, minority-group members, the physically and mentally handicapped, and the older employee. The important question is: "Who can do the job?"
4. Training opportunities, recognition for performance, overtime assignments, promotional opportunities, and all other personnel actions are to be handled on an equitable basis.

IX. IMPROVING COMMUNICATIONS
   1. Communications is achieving understanding between the sender and the receiver of a message. It also means sharing information -- the creation of understanding.
   2. Communication is basic to all human activity. Words are means of conveying meanings; however, real meanings are in people.
   3. There are very practical differences in the effectiveness of one-way, impersonal, and two-way communications. Words spoken face-to-face are better understood. Telephone conversations are effective, but lack the rapport of person-to-person exchanges. The whole person communicates.
   4. Cooperation and communication in an organization go hand-in-hand. When there is a mutual respect between people, spelling out rules and procedures for communicating is unnecessary.
   5. There are several barriers to effective communications. These include failure to listen with respect and understanding, lack of skill in feedback, and misinterpreting the meanings of words used by the speaker. It is also common practice to listen to what we want to hear, and tune out things we do not want to hear.
   6. Communication is management's chief problem. The supervisor should accept the challenge to communicate more effectively and to improve interagency and intra-agency communications.
   7. The supervisor may often plan for and conduct meetings. The planning phase is critical and may determine the success or the failure of a meeting.
   8. Speaking before groups usually requires extra effort. Stage fright may never disappear completely, but it can be controlled.

X. SELF-DEVELOPMENT
   1. Every employee is responsible for his own self-development.
   2. Toastmaster and toastmistress clubs offer opportunities to improve skills in oral communications.
   3. Planning for one's own self-development is of vital importance. Supervisors know their own strengths and limitations better than anyone else.
   4. Many opportunities are open to aid the supervisor in his developmental efforts, including job assignments; training opportunities, both governmental and non-governmental -- to include universities and professional conferences and seminars.
   5. Programmed instruction offers a means of studying at one's own rate.
   6. Where difficulties may arise from a supervisor's being away from his work for training, he may participate in televised home study or correspondence courses to meet his self-development needs.

XI. TEACHING AND TRAINING
   A. The Teaching Process
      Teaching is encouraging and guiding the learning activities of students toward established goals. In most cases this process consists in five steps: preparation, presentation, summarization, evaluation, and application.

1. Preparation

    Preparation is twofold in nature; that of the supervisor and the employee.

    Preparation by the supervisor is absolutely essential to success. He must know what, when, where, how, and whom he will teach. Some of the factors that should be considered are:

    (1) The objectives
    (2) The materials needed
    (3) The methods to be used
    (4) Employee participation
    (5) Employee interest
    (6) Training aids
    (7) Evaluation
    (8) Summarization

    Employee preparation consists in preparing the employee to receive the material. Probably the most important single factor in the preparation of the employee is arousing and maintaining his interest. He must know the objectives of the training, why he is there, how the material can be used, and its importance to him.

2. Presentation

    In presentation, have a carefully designed plan and follow it. The plan should be accurate and complete, yet flexible enough to meet situations as they arise. The method of presentation will be determined by the particular situation and objectives.

3. Summary

    A summary should be made at the end of every training unit and program. In addition, there may be internal summaries depending on the nature of the material being taught. The important thing is that the trainee must always be able to understand how each part of the new material relates to the whole.

4. Application

    The supervisor must arrange work so the employee will be given a chance to apply new knowledge or skills while the material is still clear in his mind and interest is high. The trainee does not really know whether he has learned the material until he has been given a chance to apply it. If the material is not applied, it loses most of its value.

5. Evaluation

    The purpose of all training is to promote learning. To determine whether the training has been a success or failure, the supervisor must evaluate this learning.

    In the broadest sense evaluation includes all the devices, methods, skills, and techniques used by the supervisor to keep himself and the employees informed as to their progress toward the objectives they are pursuing. The extent to which the employee has mastered the knowledge, skills, and abilities, or changed his attitudes, as determined by the program objectives, is the extent to which instruction has succeeded or failed.

    Evaluation should not be confined to the end of the lesson, day, or program but should be used continuously. We shall note later the way this relates to the rest of the teaching process.

B. Teaching Methods

   A teaching method is a pattern of identifiable student and instructor activity used in presenting training material.

   All supervisors are faced with the problem of deciding which method should be used at a given time.

1. Lecture
   The lecture is direct oral presentation of material by the supervisor. The present trend is to place less emphasis on the trainer's activity and more on that of the trainee.
2. Discussion
   Teaching by discussion or conference involves using questions and other techniques to arouse interest and focus attention upon certain areas, and by doing so creating a learning situation. This can be one of the most valuable methods because it gives the employees an opportunity to express their ideas and pool their knowledge.
3. Demonstration
   The demonstration is used to teach how something works or how to do something. It can be used to show a principle or what the results of a series of actions will be. A well-staged demonstration is particularly effective because it shows proper methods of performance in a realistic manner.
4. Performance
   Performance is one of the most fundamental of all learning techniques or teaching methods. The trainee may be able to tell how a specific operation should be performed but he cannot be sure he knows how to perform the operation until he has done so.

As with all methods, there are certain advantages and disadvantages to each method.

5. Which Method to Use
   Moreover, there are other methods and techniques of teaching. It is difficult to use any method without other methods entering into it. In any learning situation a combination of methods is usually more effective than any one method alone.

Finally, evaluation must be integrated into the other aspects of the teaching-learning process.
It must be used in the motivation of the trainees; it must be used to assist in developing understanding during the training; and it must be related to employee application of the results of training.
This is distinctly the role of the supervisor.

Facts About Golf Course Pesticides
From the Golf Course Superintendents Association of America

---

1. Why do golf courses use pesticides?

Pesticides help to limit the damage that can be caused by insects, weeds and plant diseases. Insecticides, herbicides and fungicides are used very selectively to protect the health of turf, trees and other living things on the course. Fertilizers provide much-needed nutrition for the course's plant life.

It is very important to note that the pesticides and fertilizers are not used primarily for aesthetic reasons. First and foremost, they are tools that help ensure a healthy playing surface for the game. Furthermore, they help to protect a valuable and ecologically important piece of land. Golf courses are tremendous economic assets as well as vital greenspaces for communities. They employ hundreds of thousands of people, enhance local economies through tax revenues and tourism and provide many ecological benefits. For example, golf courses help to filter air pollutants and create fresh oxygen, they are excellent groundwater recharge sites and, most importantly, they are critical wildlife sanctuaries in urban and suburban areas.

2. How does a superintendent decide when to apply a pesticide?

Pest problems on golf courses are often relatively predictable or can be diagnosed as part of an ongoing monitoring program. Once the problem has been identified, the superintendent considers the available options. These could include cultural practices (such as physically removing weeds, changing irrigation patterns or clearing underbrush around a problem area to allow more air movement) or the use of biological controls or chemical products. Once the problem is diagnosed and the right treatment has been selected, the superintendent waits for the ideal time to treat the problem in the most effective and environmentally sound manner available. This approach is often called "integrated pest management."

3. What kinds of products are used?

Most people are surprised to find that the majority of the pesticide products used by superintendents are identical or closely related to those used by homeowners.

4. How do we know that these products aren't harmful to humans or wildlife?

Pesticide production is one of the most highly regulated industries in the United States. Before a product is registered by the EPA, it must be rigorously tested for potential human health and environmental effects. This process can take up to ten years and involve more than 120 different tests and studies. Today, manufacturers often invest up to $50 million in product safety and testing before a new pesticide ever comes to the market.

5. Are golfers at risk?

No. There is no scientific evidence that golfers face any chronic health risks from the pesticides used to maintain courses. Once a liquid product is applied and the turfgrass is dry or the product has been watered in, there is very little chance of exposure to golfers or others who enter the area. It is worth noting that a small percentage of people may be allergic to a particular product, just as some people are allergic to household cleaners, soaps or perfumes. Golfers with possible chemical allergies are always encouraged to contact superintendents to find out what products might be in use.

6. If the products aren't that dangerous, why do professional applicators wear protective gear?

Applicators work directly with pesticides and are exposed much more often than golfers. Consider the fact that it is safe for a person to have an occasional x-ray, but the technician may actually leave the room to prevent repeated exposure. Pesticide label directions (which carry the weight of law) require that applicators take certain precautions based on the assumption that the same person will be repeatedly exposed to the same product over many years. These precautions may include the use of rubber gloves, goggles, respirators or protective clothing.

7. Some media stories suggest that pesticides are linked to cancer. What are the facts?

Most of the product testing required by EPA focuses on this question. Before a product is registered, tests are done (usually on laboratory rats) using exposure rates that are considerably higher than any exposure a golfer could ever receive. Although a recent study commissioned by GCSAA to examine causes of death among its members found some higher rates of certain cancers, researchers said that no cause-and-effect relationship could be established from the data. They also said that lifestyle choices (smoking, diet, stress, etc.) were the most significant factor in the results.

8. Do properly applied chemicals pose a threat to groundwater, lakes or streams?

No. Studies consistently show that a well-managed golf course can actually improve water quality on and around the facility. Research also shows that when pesticides and fertilizers are used properly, they do not tend to seep into groundwater or run off into surface water. Modern products and practices allow superintendents to manage turfgrass so efficiently that there is little chance of harm to our precious water resources.

9. What kinds of training and education do superintendents and golf course applicators have?

Golfers are often surprised to find that most superintendents have college degrees in agronomy, horticulture or a related field. Because it's important to keep up-to-date with new information and technologies, the majority also attend continuing education programs offered by universities and associations like GCSAA. Superintendents are widely considered to be among the best-educated and most judicious users of pesticide products. The vast majority of superintendents are using integrated pest management practices to ensure that both the turf and the environment stay healthy. Applicators are also trained and licensed by the state. A recent study indicated that nearly 100 percent of GCSAA-member courses had at least one licensed applicator on staff (despite the fact that it isn't necessarily required in some states). This confirms a high degree of compliance and concern about safe and proper usage of chemical tools.

Anyone with a question about golf course pesticide practices is encouraged to talk with their local superintendent or call the GCSAA at 913/841-2240 to find out more.

GLOSSARY OF GOLF TERMS

A

ACE
A hole played in one stroke. Hole-in-one.

ADDRESS
Position when a player has taken his stance preparatory to hitting ball.

AMATEUR
One who plays golf as a sport without compensation. (See USGA Policy on Amateur Status)

APPROACH
Shot to green; area in front of green.

APRON
Area immediately bordering green, generally mowed about halfway between green and fairway height.

AWAY
Ball farthest from hole and to be played next.

B

BACK DOOR
When ball rims cup and drops from back.

BACKSPIN
Backward spin of ball after being struck.

BAIL OUT
One-putting to redeem a poor hole.

BALL
To meet USGA legal specifications, a golf ball must not be smaller than 1.68 inches in diameter, weigh not more than 1.62 ounces, and travel not faster than 255 feet per second when tested at 75 degrees temperature on the USGA's velocity apparatus. British rules permit ball to be as small as 1.62 inches in diameter, with same weight as United States ball.

BANANA BALL
Slice; shot that starts left and fades right. (From right to left for left-handed player)

BEST-BALL
Term commonly used for four-ball match.

BINGLE-BANGLE-BUNGLE
A game. (See kinds of golf games)

BIRDIE
One stroke under par.

BISQUE
Handicap stroke that may be taken on any hole at option of recipient.

BLAST
Explosion shot out of sand.

BLIND BOGEY
Competition in which players, before teeing off, estimate handicaps required to net them scores between 70 and 80. A *blind* figure in this range is then selected and player with closest net is declared winner.

BLIND HOLE
 One on which green is hidden from view and cannot be seen when approaching it.

BOBS AND BIRDS
 A game. (See kinds of golf games)

BOGEY
 In United States, commonly refers to score of one above par on a hole. In other countries, it refers to score average person should be able to make on a hole, with par and bogey being the same on some easier holes.

BORROW
 Allowance that must be made in line of putt when putting over slanting sections of green.

BRASSIE
 Old name for No. 2 wood.

BUNKER
 A hazard consisting of depression covered with sand. A sandtrap, or trap.

BYE
 A term used in tournament pairings. Players who draw them have no opponent in that round.

C

CADDIE
 Carries a player's bag and may give advice.

CHICAGO SYSTEM
 A game. (See kinds of golf games)

CHIP SHOT
 Short approach shot of low trajectory.

COURSE RATING
 A rating in strokes of the play difficulty of a course. Rating is done by an association to provide the basis for uniform handicapping irrespective of course difficulty.

CUT SHOT
 Outside-in swing at ball with lofted club.

D

DIVOT
 Piece of sod that is cut away by club.

DOG-LEG
 Hole where fairway turns to left or right.

DORMIE
 When a player or side in match play is as many holes up as remain to be played.

DOWN
 When a side is behind in a match, indicated by number of holes. Opposite of Up, for ahead.

DUCK HOOK
 Right-to-left curving shot in which ball veers or hooks and drops sharply.

DUFFER
 Unskilled golfer; dub; hacker.

E

EAGLE
Two strokes under par.

EXPLOSION
Sandtrap shot in which clubface is brought into and through sand under ball; blast.

F

FAIRWAY
Closely mowed area between tee and green.

FLUSH
To hit ball with full swing precisely on clubface.

FORE
Warning cry to any and all persons who are within range of a shot. Request for silence and immobility. Its use has been ruled in courts as mitigating the liability of golfer whose ball strikes and injures a person.

FOUR-BALL
Competition in which two partners use only the better of their scores on each hole. (Also BEST BALL)

FOURSOME
A colloquialism for four golfers playing together. (Also: Threesome for three players; twosome for two) (See kinds of Sides and Matches)

FROG-HAIR
Short grass bordering edge of green.

G

GRAIN
The lie of the grass on a putting green.

GRASSCUTTER
A low, hard-hit ball that skims grass.

GREENIES
A game. (See kinds of golf games)

GROSS SCORE
Score before handicap is deducted.

H

HAZARD
A ditch, stream, lake or bunker (sandtrap).

HOLE-HIGH
A ball come to rest even with the hole.

HOLE-OUT
To finish putting.

HONOR
Right to drive or play first, determined by lowest score on preceding hole, or by other means of first tee.

L

LIE
  Position of ball on ground. Also angle between clubhead and shaft.
LINKS
  A seaside golf course.
LIP
  Edge of hole or front edge of bunker.

M

MATCH PLAY
  Two-sided competition by holes. Match ends when one side is ahead by more holes than there are holes left to play.
MEDAL PLAY
  (See STROKE PLAY)
MEDALIST
  Competitor with lowest qualifying score preceding match play.
MULLIGAN
  Second ball sometimes allowed after poor tee shot, usually on first tee. Not permitted under rules.

N

NASSAU
  A competition in which three points are scored, one for each nine and for the 18 holes. Believed to have originated at Nassau (N.Y.) CC.
NET
  Score after handicap is deducted.

O

OUT-OF-BOUNDS
  Ground on which play is prohibited.

P

PAR
  Score an expert golfer would make for a hole under ordinary weather conditions allowing two putts per hole.
PITCH SHOT
  Short approach shot of high trajectory which travels very little after it falls to the turf.
PREFERRED LIES (Winter Rules)
  Improving lie of ball, usually allowed in fairway only, by moving it a few inches with the clubhead. (See winter rules)
PRESS
  (1) Effort to apply more than normal power and hope for better than normal results from a shot; (2) An extra bet, usually on last few holes or on second nine of a Nassau wager for amount loser lost on first nine.

PUNCH SHOT
A low shot executed by punching club down at the ball. Usually played to green into heavy wind.

R

RAINMAKER
Very high shot with little distance.
RIM THE CUP
When ball circles cup without dropping.
ROUGH
Area of long grass not maintained as fairway.
ROUND-ROBIN
Tournament in which every player meets every other player one time.
RUB OF THE GREEN
This occurs when a ball in motion is stopped or deflected by an outside agency.

S

SCRATCH PLAYER
One whose handicap is zero.
SCOTCH FOURSOME
A common term for competition in which two partners play one ball, alternating strokes.
SHANK
When ball flies off neck or hosel of club.
SKY
To hit ball very high with little distance.
SNAKE
Long putt with several *borrows*.
STONY
Hitting a ball close to the hole, or *stiff*.
STROKE PLAY
Competition in which total of the hole by hole score determines the result. Medal play.
SUDDEN DEATH
When a match is tied after playing last hole, additional holes played until one player wins.

T

TEXAS WEDGE
A putter when used from chipping distance or out of a sandtrap.
TEE
Area two club lengths behind and between tee markers on which to tee ball for drive. Also a peg or other object to hold ball of the ground for tee shot.
TOE
Tip or end of clubhead.

TOP
  To strike ball on top.
WAGGLE
  Short swings of the clubhead in the process of addressing the ball prior to striking it.
WHIFF
  When player misses ball completely.

ANSWER SHEET

TEST NO. _____ PART _____ TITLE OF POSITION _____
(AS GIVEN IN EXAMINATION ANNOUNCEMENT - INCLUDE OPTION, IF ANY)

PLACE OF EXAMINATION _____ DATE _____
(CITY OR TOWN)   (STATE)

RATING

USE THE SPECIAL PENCIL. MAKE GLOSSY BLACK MARKS.

Make only ONE mark for each answer. Additional and stray marks may be counted as mistakes. In making corrections, erase errors COMPLETELY.

ANSWER SHEET

TEST NO. _____ PART _____ TITLE OF POSITION _____
(AS GIVEN IN EXAMINATION ANNOUNCEMENT - INCLUDE OPTION, IF ANY)

PLACE OF EXAMINATION _____ DATE _____
(CITY OR TOWN)   (STATE)

RATING

USE THE SPECIAL PENCIL.   MAKE GLOSSY BLACK MARKS.

Make only ONE mark for each answer.   Additional and stray marks may be counted as mistakes.   In making corrections, erase errors COMPLETELY.